the
software
revelation

What computer code can teach us
about transcendence
in a post-religious world

xavier kahn

authorHOUSE®

AuthorHouse™
1663 Liberty Drive
Bloomington, IN 47403
www.authorhouse.com
Phone: 833-262-8899

Published by AuthorHouse 12/16/2020

ISBN: 978-1-7283-7362-1 (sc)
ISBN: 978-1-7283-7360-7 (hc)
ISBN: 978-1-7283-7361-4 (e)

Library of Congress Control Number: 2020917322

For Monkey

Anecdote of the Jar

I placed a jar in Tennessee,
And round it was, upon a hill.
It made the slovenly wilderness
Surround that hill.

The wilderness rose up to it,
And sprawled around, no longer wild.
The jar was round upon the ground
And tall and of a port in air.

It took dominion everywhere.
The jar was gray and bare.
It did not give of bird or bush,
Like nothing else in Tennessee.

–Wallace Stevens

Contents

PART III: RELATIONALITY
(a/k/a THE SPACES BETWEEN STUFF)

PART IV: OUR RUNTIME NARRATIVES

PART V: NARRATIVES OF THE DIVINE

PART VI: SO WHAT?
(a/k/a POTENTIAL IMPLICATIONS OF
THE SOFTWARE REVELATION)

Why read this book?

This book is about software. It's also about something more.

Humankind has always grappled with this something more, which for our purposes we'll call the "transcendent." Prophets and poets have tried to describe it. Temples have been built to exalt it. Art has been created to express it. And we've all experienced it—whether in a heart-stopping sunset or in the simple delight of being with a loved one.

In the wake of the Scientific Revolution and a European intellectual movement known as "The Enlightenment," however, a kind of metaphysical schizophrenia has impaired our engagement with the transcendent. That's because we've come to view the transcendent as though it were an entirely separate realm from what we'll call the "tangible."

The tangible realm encompasses the physical universe, including our physical selves. It's the realm we learn about through direct observation and scientific experimentation. The marvelous results of the empirical methods we employ to explore this tangible realm include our abilities to cure diseases, to chart the stars, and to conveniently zap frozen cheeseburgers in our microwaves.

Meanwhile, we've exiled the transcendent to an entirely separate realm. This is the realm where we engage with matters such as love, goodness, evil, beauty, justice, and our sense of place in the cosmos. These transcendent matters don't readily yield themselves to the empirical knowledge-gathering methods we apply to the tangible—yet they are nonetheless quite real and quite integral to our lived experience. The transcendent may resist quantitative measurement in our laboratories and observation through our telescopes, but it persists in our consciousness as it continues to inspire us, befuddle us, and pique our curiosity.

Because our engagements with the tangible and the transcendent have diverged so much over the centuries, we've developed a bad habit of applying quite different vocabularies to them—granting one the exclusive right to be deemed "rational" and "objective," while dismissing the other as merely a matter of personal faith or opinion. This metaphysical schizophrenia—formally referred to as "dualism"—stigmatizes the transcendent as somehow immune to reason, while at the same time tempting us to overestimate our capacity to fully grasp the deeper, more intransigent mysteries of the tangible.

This book offers a possible way out of our metaphysically schizophrenic dualism and the various associated ailments of narrative we tend to suffer as a result. Muons and music, after all, inhabit a single shared cosmos. So in the following pages, we'll try to uniformly apply our rational capacities to *both* the tangible *and* the transcendent.

More specifically, we'll take advantage of the phenomenon of software—a phenomenon that has so recently and so quickly become pervasively present in our lives—to consider:

- Whether there can be observable *agency* (that is, the ability to participate in causation) without an inherently observable *agent*.
- Whether the attributes that endow software with its agency—including abstraction, instantiation, "chunking," and relationality—reveal anything about the cosmos more generally.

- Whether the agency and identity of entities in the cosmos (including ourselves) are based more on the _relationships between them_ than on any attributes inherent in entities themselves.
- Whether the relationship-centricity revealed by software can help us better understand our cosmos and ourselves in some new, useful, and unified way.

If you avidly embrace the transcendent, this book may help you better ground your beliefs in reason. If you're someone who tends to shy away from anything that smacks of transcendence, on the other hand, this book may open you to the possibility that human knowledge is not strictly bounded by the limits of the scientific method—and that rational investigation of the transcendent is in fact essential to any coherent understanding of our universe and ourselves.

Regardless of your current views, I hope you find the ideas here helpful and thought-provoking. There is much that software can reveal to us. This is my attempt to share some of those revelations with you.

Enjoy!

–Xavier Kahn, October 2020

PART I:
THE SOFTWARE REVELATION

1

Why software?

Why a book about software and transcendence? And why now?

To answer that question, we need only consider two simple facts:

1) Software is everywhere, affecting everything.
2) Software doesn't exist—at least not in the way we normally think of existence.

We are the first generation of humans for whom this combination of seemingly contradictory truths—that software can *do* so much without observably *being*—is so palpably evident. Software dominates our work, our leisure, our society, and our world. We use software constantly on phones and computers, in our cars, at store kiosks and ATMs. I used software to write this book, and software delivered it into your hands. We're even starting to understand the universe itself in terms of software—such as when we speak of genetic "code" or try to understand the most fundamental laws of matter and energy.

Yet no one has ever directly observed software itself. That's because software is not directly observable. You can't see it or take a picture of it. You can see what it does—and, yes, you can see the letters, numbers, and symbols that programmers use to build applications. But, as we'll consider in more detail later, none of that is software itself. Trying to observe software is like trying to put a laugh in a bottle.

So what? Why should anybody care about the fact that software is both everywhere and nowhere? Isn't this just some quirky metaphysical question for philosophy students?

I don't think it is. Anthropology, sociology, and psychology all teach us that our foundational beliefs about the universe (i.e., our metaphysics) affect us profoundly. If one of my fundamental beliefs is that I have a soul that manifests as an animal spirit assigned to me at birth, then that belief will strongly influence how I relate to the natural world and to those who identify with the same particular animal spirit as I do.

If, on the other hand, I fundamentally believe that the blood running through my veins makes me the rightful heir to the French throne, I'll relate to people and the world much differently.

Likewise, if deep down we believe the universe boils down to some basic unit of "stuff"—observable hardware, if you will—then we're likely to see ourselves as "stuff" too. That idea (which we will consider later as "reductive materialism") will, in turn, affect how we think, live, and interact.

The core idea of this book is that we can seize on this special moment in human history—this moment when the realities of software are becoming evident to everyone, rather than just a small priesthood of technologists—to re-think our fundamental beliefs about the universe and ourselves.

Such re-thinking has occurred periodically during times of intense change in our lived experience. It happened when we started farming thousands of years ago. It happened with the advent of the printing press, during the Scientific and Industrial Revolutions, and after the cataclysm of world war. It makes sense that the tremendous changes taking place in our lives due to the pervasiveness of software would lead to another major historical re-thinking now.

So what does software reveal? How could those revelations affect the way we think and live?

To answer these questions, we'll first examine what software is and how it works. Then we'll consider the metaphysical implications of software's attributes in the clear light of reason.

But in case you need a little motivation to wade through the technical material in these opening chapters, here's a clue. Our investigation will suggest that it's not especially rational to restrict our understanding of the universe and ourselves to the "stuff" we can observe with our senses and with the clever devices we build. In fact, software reveals that it's quite *ir*rational to restrict ourselves in this way.

By better understanding what software is and how it works, I believe we can find evidence that it is fully rational to embrace truths about the universe and about ourselves that we may rightly term "transcendent." These truths are outside the observational limits of scientific inquiry—but they are nevertheless well within the reach of the very same human reason that enables us to do science in the first place.

All we need to do is apply that reason to the revelations newly afforded us by the ubiquitous, world-changing phenomenon of software.

What is software?

First, let's define "software." For our purposes here, we're going to define software as "values in relationship to each other."[1]

"Values in relationship to each other" is a good working definition for software because it concisely describes what software developers produce when they write code—and how software works when it runs on hardware.

The computer software you and I use every day employs only the two most basic values: 0 and 1. Because it only employs these two values, we often refer to this kind of software as "binary code."

The software programmer's job is to place these 0 and 1 values in a very specific relationship to each other—that relationship being a particular order or sequence—so the software does what it's intended to do. Then, when it's time to run the software, a hardware device processes those 0 and 1 values in their properly ordered sequence.

The word-processing software I'm using right now to create this book on my laptop is comprised of nothing but such 0s and 1s. So is the software that's enabling you to read these words on a digital screen (if that's how you're reading this) or to post a scathing

---

[1] I'll ask for license to freely substitute words such as "code," "application," "app," and "program" for "software," since most of us use them somewhat interchangeably anyway—and different words fit better in different contexts.

critique of this book on social media (if you'd like to give this book some free publicity).

In fact, countless zillions of 0s and 1s are streaming through digital devices and across digital networks at an unfathomable rate all over the world at this very moment—connecting people, executing transactions, and streaming video. Software can do all this because we have built the global digital infrastructure to rapidly deliver specific sets of 0s and 1s in very precise sequence to millions of computing devices.

More than just apps

There are several reasons why I prefer to define software as "values in relationship to each other," rather than, say, "a sequence of 0s and 1s that give instructions to computers." These reasons include:

1) **Software doesn't have to be binary.** We use 0s and 1s in general computing because our underlying hardware primarily uses electronics that ultimately have to be either "off" or "on." That's why our most basic unit of information is known as a "bit" (short for "binary digit").[2]

   But there's no reason to limit our definition of software to binary code alone. In hexadecimal code, for example, each sequential value can range from 1 to 16. Genetic code uses four different values in the form of the nucleotides adenine (A), cytosine (C), guanine (G), and either uracil (U) or thymine (T). The written English language can be understood as a code of 26 letter-values—plus sundry

---

[2] Because a bit is such a small unit of information, it's not very useful for measuring the capacity of computing systems. That's why we instead use a "byte," which is 8 bits. To get a little geekier about it, a byte can encode more than eight times as much information as a bit—because there are 256 (or 2^8) possible combinations of eight 0s and 1s. Try it yourself and you'll see.

punctuations marks—that I'm placing in a certain sequence at this very moment to write this book.

Code, in other words, doesn't have to be binary—or even numerical. Its only fundamental requirements are that it utilize *values* and that it place those values in some type of well-defined *relationship to each other*.

2) **Software is more than just instructions.** While software developers generally write code to execute a set of specific intended actions, we don't have to limit our definition of software to intentional instructions alone.

For one thing, software is still software even if it doesn't work quite right. A bad programmer may write buggy code—but it's still code.

For another, the data files, documents, pictures, and videos stored on our computers can also be considered "code" even though we might not think of them as containing programmatic instructions. They're still sets of values in an ordered relationship to each other. It's just that such files are a static form of code that stores information—such as a financial statement or a musical performance—rather than active code that can execute a specific set of actions, such as running a navigation app.

Furthermore, the software we create for artificial intelligence (AI), machine learning (ML), and other related disciplines isn't really "program code" as we've historically understood it. AI and ML define methods for handling data—but they aren't restricted by preset instructions of conventional line-by-line software routines. The dynamic, self-modifying capabilities of AI and ML allow code to keep adapting itself automatically over time (i.e. changing its own values in relationship to each other) so it can continuously optimize the measurable outcomes or results it produces.

So rather than tying our definition of "software" to any notions of intention or action, we're probably better off whittling that definition down to a simple description of its core attributes: values and their positional relationships to each other.

3) **Software isn't limited to computers.** As the examples of genetic code and language illustrate, software doesn't necessarily have to run on a computer. Computer code is certainly teaching us more than ever about software because computing has become so pervasive. And it's precisely because computing has become so pervasive that a life-long technologist like me can finally write a book about software for non-technical readers. Even the least geeky among us now have enough direct experience with software that a book about it can (hopefully!) appeal to a broad audience.

But software as we're defining it here existed way before we ever had computers. Recipes are a kind of software. Musical compositions are a kind of software. Computer programming has simply enabled us to more systematically and extensively harness the power of an underlying principle—values in relationship—that has always been present in the universe.

Of course, not everyone will accept "values in relationship with each other" as the ideal definition of software. But I'm hoping you can at least tolerate the definition long enough to get something worthwhile out of this book.

3

How software works: Encoding

If software is nothing but a bunch of values, how is it capable of doing anything? What is it about code that has made it such a powerful force in the world—in how we buy and sell, in how we do science and art, in how we interact with friends and family?

There are several ways to describe how software works. One useful approach is to first look at how software *en*codes and then look at how software is *de*coded—that is, how it "runs."

Let's start with encoding first. One way to describe software encoding is *unitized abstraction*. Here's what I mean by each of those terms:

Unitization

To "unitize" in this context means to express something in value units.[3] In the case of computer software, programmers express large, complex tasks using sequences of the value units 0 and 1. Programmers generally don't do this all in one fell swoop. Programmers perform unitization by a process we'll call "chunking" that first breaks the overall objective into smaller, more manageable pieces—and then

---

[3] "Unitize" can also mean to "unify"—as in bringing otherwise scattered things together. But we're not going to use the word in that sense here.

further breaks down those smaller pieces into even smaller sets of individual values in relationship to each other.

A navigation app, for example, helps you get where you're going by "chunking" that overall challenge into discrete parts: determining your present location via GPS coordinates, correlating that location to a road map, processing the data you input for your destination, analyzing the available routes between those two points based on a certain set of parameters, displaying that route, and so on.

It's worth noting that as software has become more complex, developers have gotten better and better at "chunking." In the software industry, we've used terms like "containers" and "microservices" to describe functional chunks of code—but the idea is basically the same: break something complex down into smaller pieces that are broken down into still smaller pieces until ultimately everything is expressed in the value units 0 and 1.

Chunking enables us to re-use code someone else has already built. Suppose, for example, you were writing software for a bowling robot. You'd need some kind of formula to compute how the bowling ball's spin affects its motion over the surface of a bowling lane. If you chunked that formula (or put it in a "container" or architected it as a "microservice") you could re-purpose the associated code if you wanted your robot to shoot pool or play soccer. That way, you wouldn't have to constantly re-do all the work of unitizing the complex math required to calculate the effect of ball's spin on its movement over a surface into 0s and 1s. That spin-effect would already be chunked as a functional ready-made software module.

This chunking technique is also what makes the amazing effects achieved in computer animation possible. If movie animators want to depict a thousand hairy aliens descending upon Los Angeles, they don't have to code every single hair on every single alien separately. They chunk the hairs and chunk the aliens so they can rapidly multiply the invading horde to whatever size they desire by simply repeating the chunks with certain coded variations.

Even when software developers don't have any prefabricated chunks of code available that already do what they need to do, they don't sit at their desks typing out millions of 0s and 1s. Instead, they use programming languages and graphical tools that enable them to describe what they want their code to do in logical terms—"use these variables in this formula," "color the pixels in this object with this shade of blue," etc.—and then they feed those descriptions written in that programming language to another type of program (called a "compiler") that converts the logic of their programming-language descriptions into the 0s and 1s that conventional computing hardware requires.

Regardless of how any particular programmer chooses to write code, *unitization* is how software encapsulates even the most complex application logic into a finite set of values—whether those values are 0s and 1s, a handful of amino acids, or the twelve tones of the western musical scale.

Abstraction

"Abstraction" refers to the correlation or correspondence programmers create between objects, attributes, and actions in the "real world" and their associated representations in unitized code. This translation into code can also be described as "digitization" or "virtualization."

Let's consider as an example how I, Xavier Kahn, might be abstracted into unitized code by one of the many companies I order from online. As a human being, I'm a pretty complex entity. Biologically, I'm comprised of millions of cells organized into numerous organs and systems. I also possess an individual identity that includes my life history, family relationships, emotional idiosyncrasies, and killer moves on the dance floor.

The companies with which I interact, however, don't translate the entire Xavier Kahn person we know and love into code. Instead, the software these companies use simply assign me a customer ID, which abstracts Xavier Kahn's existence into an alphanumeric string—i.e. a set of values in a specific sequence.

Those letters and numbers don't have to describe anything about me, although for convenience my customer ID may start with "K," include a numerical code identifying me as a resident of a particular geographical region, and/or tag me as one of the company's premium customers. Whatever system the company uses to create its customer IDs, however, that ID is an _abstraction_ of my identity. It is not the real me.

A company's software can then attach attributes—my gender, my address, my last purchase, etc.—to my abstracted identity in a database, which is simply a way to organize chunks of code. But even those attributes are unitized (i.e., converted into binary code) and abstracted. Instead of identifying my last purchase as the ugly Christmas sweater I bought for my younger son because I love sending goofy gifts, for example, it will probably abstract the sweater as an alphanumeric SKU (an abbreviation of "stock-keeping unit"). That SKU may not contain any information about the sweater's ugliness or appropriateness for winter wear. It is simply an abstraction of a particular product in code.

Abstraction is thus the means by which the tangible is translated into code—or, perhaps more precisely, into chunks of code that are in turn comprised of unitized binary code.

▪ ▪ ▪

Putting these two concepts together, we have _unitized abstraction_. "Unitized" refers to the use of a finite set of values placed in a particular sequence as the underlying language of the code. "Abstraction" refers to the representational function of that code.

The power of software thus arises in part from unitized abstraction, which enables software to possess well-defined correlations to the tangible. This correlation is the essence of encoding.

4

How software works: Running the code

Encoding endows software with the *potential* ability to do something (what I earlier referred to as "agency"). That potential, however, is only realized when the software actually runs—or is *de*coded—on a piece of hardware.

To describe how hardware runs software, I'll suggest another word-pair: *ordered instantiation*. Bear with me as I explain what I mean by each of those words:

Ordered

I'm using the word "ordered" to denote the fact that the relationships between the values in a piece of software created during encoding must be preserved when the software is run. Preservation of order is critical to software execution. When software runs on your computer, every 0 and 1 (that is, every electronic charge and not-charge) must pass through a microscopic labyrinth of logic gates, storage media, and interconnections in the precisely correct order. If it doesn't, your computer freezes or fails to render a web page correctly or tells you that 2 + 2 = 1.400087129336518e+19.

Computers use mechanisms such as CHECKSUM to continuously validate both the values and the sequence of those values as they pass through its hardware. The imperative of order is also why your computer's performance is constrained by clockspeed—the fastest rate at which its processor can read 0s and 1s in their proper sequence—rather than by the pure speed with which electronic impulses could theoretically move across physical media (i.e., the speed of light).

Order doesn't only refer to the proper sequencing of the 0s and 1s running through a chip's logic gates. It also refers to how larger chunks of code relate to each other. A line of code somewhere in an application can tell a computer to run a section of code elsewhere in that program. It can even tell the computer to run a section of code in an entirely different program. Once that "called" section runs, the code has to tell the computer to go back to where it left off before it ran the "called" section—or to move on to some other entirely different section of code. The integrity of this "calling" between chunks of code depends on well-ordered relationships between the 0s and 1s within and between programs.

Order is not only critical for software to run properly on a given computer. It's also critical to ensure the integrity of communication *between* computers. The awesomeness of the Internet is at least partially attributable to its transmission protocols, which make sure that devices can accurately send order-dependent code over a network to each other—even if some of that code gets a little jumbled up as it zips across the Internet's complex, dynamic infrastructure.

This preservation of order is achieved by breaking down large quantities of transmitted 0s and 1s into small packets (another good example of chunking). These packets are comprised of two parts: the code actually being transmitted (the "payload") and supplementary code that provides instructions on how to route the code-packet across the network and how to process it at the receiving end (the "header"). It's as if you mailed a 100-page document to someone in ten different envelopes—each marked Envelope #1, Envelope #2, etc.

To ensure the security of your code-packets as they traverse the network, you can even encrypt them. Encryption distorts the 0s and 1s in your message using a very specific algorithm. Only your intended recipient has this algorithm (or "key") which allows them to decrypt the code—that is, restore the 0s and 1s to their original order.

"Ordered" is also a good antonym for "chaos." By emphasizing the requirement that software executes in a properly _ordered_ manner, we're specifically contrasting software's behavior from chaos or randomness—as well as from improperly ordered relationships between the values in chunks of code.

Instantiation

Technologists often refer to any particular copy of a piece of software at some place and/or time as an "instance." If you and I are both using the exact same version of the same web browser, for example, then we each have an "instance" of that exact same browser software on our computers.

I'm using "instantiation" in somewhat the same sense. For software to do anything anywhere in the world, it must be instantiated somewhere. However, it's not enough for the software to just sit idly on some device's hard drive—as, say, your word-processing application is before you open it and start writing. For software to do something, at least some portion of its code must be _active_ on a device. This state of activity is known as "execution" or "runtime."

So for our purposes, "instantiation" refers to the entire lifecycle of any individual instance of code—including its installation, storage, linking, loading, and ultimate execution.

Execution of a software instance can occur locally—such as when your personal local instance of your computer's calculator program runs right there on your own computer. But that's just one model of instantiation. Back in the 1970's, I'd sit at a so-called "dumb" terminal. We call them "dumb" because they didn't have any ability whatsoever to run software. All they did was send my keystrokes to an instance of code running on a distant mainframe—and then noisily print out the results of what the code did on that distant mainframe onto a roll of paper mounted on my terminal.

When PCs became popular in the 80's and 90's, we began using a similar model we called "client-server." Under this model, you could run some software on your desktop computer—but if you were in an office, you'd also run some software on your company's servers, which were more powerful computers located in a computer room. This model offered the best of both worlds: the speed of local execution when appropriate and access to the power needed to run more complex application code when necessary.

Nowadays, we use a model of remote instantiation that we call the "cloud." While the term "cloud" is technically used to describe a variety of computing architectures,[4] it has become popular as shorthand for any situation where the software you use is running on some pool of computer hardware sitting somewhere in a data center owned and operated by someone else—such as Amazon, Microsoft, or Apple.

Many companies avoid the maintenance burdens and costs associated with installing, running, managing, and securing the complex software they need for sales, marketing, and/or human resources on their own in-house computers by offloading those burdens and costs to a cloud-based software service provider. This cloud provider runs the software for the company in some large, highly specialized datacenter staffed with the necessary IT professionals. The companies' employees simply access the cloud provider's instance of the software via the desktop computers in their offices and/or from their smartphones.

---

[4] I.e., public clouds, private off-premise and on-premise clouds, hybrid clouds, etc.

Under this cloud computing model, individual employees' devices only have to perform the light work of 1) sending the individual employees' keystrokes and mouse-clicks to the hard-working computers in the distant datacenter and 2) displaying whatever those distant computers tell them to display on their screens. In this scenario, we say that the software is being run remotely, rather than locally. It's very similar to what I did those many years ago on the mainframe—except now we can be vastly more flexible when it comes to the remote software we use and the remote computing facilities where that software runs.

Sometimes, related code runs on both our local devices (PC, phone, tablet, wearable, or whatever) and multiple remote machines. Under this hybrid model, developers have decided that different chunks of code that perform different functions should be instantiated either locally or remotely for a variety of reasons—performance, cost, security, etc. Here again, chunking is very useful because it facilitates the logical division of computing "labor" across multiple computers in multiple locations.

To make instantiation even more interesting, we should note that software no longer has to even run directly on physical computer hardware. Instead, we have created a specialized type of code designed to emulate the workings and behavior of computer hardware. This computer-emulating code is known as a "virtual machine."

Like all software, these virtual machines run on physical computing hardware. But they're not inflexibly tied to one particular computer. Virtual machines—i.e. emulated computers made of nothing but code—can easily be moved from one physical computer to another as necessary to satisfy escalating demand, to improve performance, or to fulfill some other objective. In other words, an instance of program code can run on an instance of virtual machine code running on hardware.

All of these examples underscore that the principle of instantiation is *entirely independent of the particular means by which any code is instantiated.* The primary significance of instantiation is that to do anything, software must at some moment run somehow somewhere on something.

■ ■ ■

The potential for agency encoded into the *unitized abstraction* of a piece of software is thus only realized when there is some *ordered instantiation* of it. The reason you also can't run iPhone software on an Android phone is that the Android operating system doesn't instantiate iPhone software's values in a properly ordered manner. You can, however, use yet more code (i.e., a "virtual machine") to emulate an iPhone operating system's value-processing behaviors on a non-Apple device.

Your software also won't run if your computer's motherboard is fried— or if the virtual machine in the cloud where your software is being instantiated has been corrupted or is too swamped with traffic to process the incoming data packets from the network in an orderly manner.

Again, that's because instantiation only works when it's properly ordered. I used an *ordered instantiation* of my word-processing software to create a *unitized abstraction* of this book as a set of values in a specific relationship. You're then able to read this book because one or more *ordered instantiations* of software rendered those values in their proper relationship accessible and comprehensible to you. Otherwise, you would be reading 7&tgf$jskbBh#w18jdbbk;p@ instead of my wonderfully coherent and engaging prose.

However oversimplified, overcomplicated, or otherwise flawed you may find these opening chapters, my hope is that they give us a reasonably useful working explanation of what software is and how it gains its agency. With this working explanation in hand, we can go on to consider the nature of software more broadly—before then going on to consider what the nature of software may reveal about the nature of the cosmos and its inhabitants.

5

Software everywhere

The principles of *encoding* and *running* outlined in the previous two chapters don't just apply to modern computer software. Software has been around since the beginning of time and has taken many forms.

Language as code

One form of software we all use every day is language. As I write these lines, I'm encoding my thoughts into a particular variant of the English language. I do this by abstracting concepts such as "abstracting" and "concepts" using an encoding method that requires me to chunk those concepts into phrases and words that I then unitize into letters, spaces, and punctuation. If I don't think I've optimally abstracted a certain concept—or even a certain feeling about a concept—I have to modify my encoding by typing a different set of characters.

It's then up to you, the reader, to receive that particular instance of sequenced letters, spaces, and punctuation marks through your sensory apparatus and process it with the hardware of your brain and the operating system software of your mind—where (I hope) it will run in an ordered instantiation that extracts within some reasonable degree of accuracy the meaning I've attempted to convey.

Now there can be many a slip between the cup of my consciousness and the lip of yours. A misprint may scramble the order of the keystrokes I typed. I may fail as a writer (or, to put in another way, as a language programmer) to properly unitize and abstract the information I'm trying to communicate. You may misread something I wrote. Something I wrote may even trigger a thought in your mind that I never consciously intended to convey—which could work to our advantage or disadvantage.[5]

If you're not reading this book in English, then someone has "compiled" this book's code for your language's "operating system." You may also be visually challenged in a way that keeps you from reading this book the way I typed it. But if someone "compiles" this book in Braille, you'll be able to read it through another "operating system" anyway.

The same thing happens with speech. If you're listening to an audiobook, the reader has re-encoded my writing into a series of mouth-sound units. You're now using your auditory and cognitive faculties to run that code. Different units, same principle.

Regardless of how the process runs in any given instantiation, the ideas I hoped to convey in this book are being delivered to you through the software of language—software that requires me to perform the unitized abstraction of encoding and requires you to run an orderly instantiation of that code.

Genetic code

As noted earlier, genetic code is an excellent example of how software occurs in the natural world.

When we talk about "genetic code," we're talking about a set of values in relationship to each other. Unlike binary computer code

---

[5] The whole notion of how language enables us to code and decode linguistic signifiers is a fascinating field of study well beyond the scope of this book—although we will touch on it again later.

with just 0s and 1s, however, genetic code has four possible values: A, C, G, and either T or U—depending on whether the code is being expressed in DNA or mRNA, respectively.

Another important feature of genetic code is that these values are chunked into three-unit "codons." These codons abstract the manufacture of corresponding amino acids in a sequenced manner, so the codon UUA has a different functional property than the codon with the sequence UAU. A series of codons can then define a specific protein by specifying a sequence of amino acids.

These protein-production sequences are encoded in an organism's reproductive system. When an instantiation of that genetic code is then run in a well-ordered manner, the result is the manufacture of proteins that drive the construction of a new organism.

Most codons specify a particular amino acid to be used as a building block in the production of a required protein. "Start" and "stop" codons signal when one instruction set is complete and when another begins. Genetic code also includes regulatory instructions that determine where and when the synthesis of each protein should occur.

Because the coding and replication of genetic code is a complex biochemical process, it is subject to error. Values can be dropped, changed, or transposed. Genetic code is to some degree error-tolerant, because some transpositions don't affect the resulting amino acid production. GAA and GAG, for example, both produce glutamic acid. Some errors also generate "stop" signals that keep the miscoding from having any harmful effect—something akin to the CHECKSUM feature of computing.

Other miscodings create mutations that can be harmful or helpful. Sickle-cell disease, for example, occurs when a person inherits abnormal copies of the hemoglobin gene (which occurs on chromosome 11) from both parents. Mutations in viruses, on the other hand, can provide their organisms an advantage by allowing mutant strains to better evade the defenses of hosts' immune systems.

Of course, you are much more than just your genetic code. Your genetic code can express itself in many different ways, depending on environmental factors such as nutrition and exposure to infection. But many of your foundational characteristics—from the color of your eyes to your susceptibility to depression—are coded into your physical being via a four-value software language.

Mathematics

While mathematics may appear to be a special case of language, it is really a very distinct category of software. That's because mathematical assertions are inherently abstract, precise, and universal in a way that language is not.

When I write "Joe opened the red door," I could be referring to any one of several Joes. I might even be writing about a fictional Joe who only exists in a story I'm writing. The assertions that "1+1=2" or that "$E=mc^2$" are something else entirely. In those cases, I am asserting highly specific truths about reality in general.[6] And I'm making those assertions through references to abstract concepts such as "multiplying a number by itself."

Mathematical notation has lots of software-like rules and conventions. When we write the number 562, for example, we are describing a numeral as (5x100)+(6x10)+2. Even the parentheses I just used are a coded instruction to perform the multiplication operations first—and then the additions.

---

[6] Some of you math nerds may quibble with the universality of 1+1=2 in the context of certain mathematical functions, such as those involving whole-integer rounding. Point taken. We can discuss deconstruction in the context of mathematical notation when you DM me on Twitter.

The mathematician Kurt Gödel took the structured, abstract nature of mathematics to another level by assigning natural numbers to mathematical symbols. This then allowed him to express any well-formed mathematical formula as a single (though sometimes extremely long) natural number. By doing so, he was able to make some very powerful mathematical assertions about making mathematical assertions.

Mathematics is thus a rather special case of code. In fact, given that mathematics is foundational to our practice of the scientific method, viewing mathematics as a form of code has some very interesting implications. But we'll consider those later.

■ ■ ■

We can find many other examples of software all around us. Music is certainly one. Look at either a symphonic score or a paper roll for an old player piano. You'll see a series of values in sequence. In both cases, a musician took a set of musical ideas and encoded them—allowing them to be "run" at a later time by either a group of trained "decoders" or a mechanical device.

Color perception is another interesting software program. The physical properties of the surface of an object you're looking at may cause it to primarily reflect light at wavelength of around 540 nanometers. But you don't look at it and think "Aw, I love those wavelengths between 535 and 545 nm." Instead, light of that frequency stimulates the M cones in your retina in a certain way. Those M cones in turn send a signal to your brain that you experience as a particular shade of green. Color perception is thus a software program for processing the wavelengths of the visible spectrum.

Recipes are a kind of code too. You can't eat your grandmother's recipe for lasagna. In fact, her lasagna recipe may not even be written anywhere. But if you follow the software of her instructions step by step—unit by unit—you can reproduce the same edible results.

These examples illustrate that the notion of "code" applies far beyond our laptops and smartphones. Computer hardware and computer programming have put the power of software in human hands. But software is innate to existence—from the reproduction of life to the burning of the stars.

6

Is everything code?

In the previous chapter, we viewed a variety of phenomena other than computer applications—such as language, genetics, math, music, and cooking—as software. In this chapter, we're going to take a shot at asserting that the fabric of the universe itself can be understood as "code."

The software of the cosmos

From the beginnings of the Scientific Revolution, there has been a general sense that the universe has some kind of underlying order which—with the right experiments and the right mathematics—could be understood and codified. Newton's physics and Kepler's astronomy were ground-breaking exercises in using the language of mathematics to describe the code that governs the behavior of the universe.

Mendeleev's periodic table of the elements is an especially marvelous archetype of this cosmic code-detection. You and I experience oxygen as something we breathe and gold as the nice shiny stuff we wear as jewelry. Mendeleev looked at the findings of earlier scientists regarding the properties of these elements and discerned in them an underlying system by which they could be coherently organized.

Mendeleev accomplished this by using unitized values (i.e., atomic weight) to place all the elements that comprise the universe in a precise relationship to each other. The values-in-relationship code that Mendeleev discovered in the nature of matter didn't just help us more coherently organize the elements we'd already discovered. His code also enabled us to predict the existence of elements *before* we discovered them in nature—and to create entirely new synthetic elements in our laboratories.

The work of Einstein and other theoretical physicists can be similarly viewed as a decoding of the cosmos using the abstractions of mathematics. In Einstein's case, the "coding rules" of math and physics enabled him to make assertions about the cosmos without any experimental foundation at all. It was only sometime later—when our experimental capabilities advanced to the point that his assertions about time, space, gravity, and the like could be tested empirically—that his theories about the cosmic code were scientifically validated.

In fact, as subatomic physics continues to progress, it increasingly resembles an investigation of values within a system of coding—rather than an enterprise of discovery-by-experiment. As has been the case with amino acids in genetic code and elements in the periodic table, theoretical physicists attempt to describe physical reality with an ordering of finite values—although those values are nearly impossible for the uninitiated to understand.

Quarks, for example, are classified into six "flavors" that have been rather oddly named: up, down, strange, charm, bottom, and top. And those values cannot even be observed directly. Instead, their value-coded properties are deduced from the directly observed behaviors of the hadrons (protons, neutrons, etc.) they comprise.

Things get even more software-like with string theory, supersymmetry, and other attempts to discern whatever next level of code might lie beneath the "chunk" of abstraction we already understand. As theoretical physics keeps peeling back the cosmic onion, it continues to reduce higher-order values to more fundamental ones—just as higher-level software languages are unitized into lower-level chunks until there is ultimately a binary instruction set of 0s and 1s for the logic gates of a processor.

Quantum physics in particular tends to promote the notion of a cosmos made up of ordered values, rather than as the particles of "stuff" our human perception inclines us towards. Yes, we can observe the properties of "stuff" when it suits a purpose such as building a more efficient solar panel or a more lightweight structural material. But quantum physics also tells us that we have to put aside our particle prejudices and embrace the wave paradigm when presented with other aspects of the tangible cosmos. And waves, of course, are themselves a type of software—since they are defined exclusively by values (i.e. probability amplitudes) that are well-ordered in mathematical equations (e.g. Klein-Gordon).

We'll look at quantum theory again later in this regard. But for now, suffice to say that while theoretical physicists remain engaged in a lively debate about the fundamental nature of everything, that nature invariably looks less like "stuff" and more like a set of ordered mathematical values. In fact, recent work in quantum computing demonstrates that the fundamental nature of the cosmos may itself offer a transformative platform for running our own man-made computer programs.[7]

The first program

Of course, for the universe to be some sort of runnable/decodable program, it must have been somehow been encoded. And here the scientific community is again generally in agreement. The nature of the present known universe was fully "programmed" into it at its inception.

---

[7] For more information on this fascinating topic, you can do some research online—or get a copy of *Quantum Computation and Quantum Information* by Nielsen and Chuang.

There's no universal agreement on the specifics of this initial programming, which is closely related to the so-called "Big Bang" theory. Opinions differ significantly about specific aspects of the Big Bang—such as initial inflation, possible cyclicality, and other particulars. But all those conflicting opinions have one thing in common: They must all pass the litmus test of being able to explain why the universe exists as it does now.

That is, all narratives regarding cosmological origin are of necessity "reverse engineered"—much as a hacker might reverse-engineer a software application based on its observable behavior in order to suss out its underlying code.

Any reverse-engineered theory about the origin of the cosmos must be consistent with the "macro" attributes of the universe as it exists today: why it is topologically flat, why its temperature is so consistent everywhere, why certain elements are abundant while others are rare, etc. Any theory about the universe's original coding must also be consistent with its "micro" attributes as well: why elemental particles behave the way they do, why nucleogenesis occurs the way it does, etc.

It is those macro and micro attributes that led to the formation of the various types of galaxies and stars we can observe today. And it is the formation of those galaxies and stars that led to the formation of the various solar systems and planets we can observe today and may observe in the future. And it is the formation of those solar systems and planets that led first to the potential for life and then to the emergence of actual life on planets—specifically, in our case, the carbon-based life-forms we have on this planet called Earth, which is third from the star we call the Sun or Sol.

Finally, to bring things full circle, it is the emergence of particular carbon-based life-forms on our home planet Earth that led to the evolution of life intelligent enough to observe the universe and attempt to decode it.

Consciousness itself, in other words, was coded into the Big Bang.

A variety of thinkers have weighed in on how the eventual emergence of beings capable of both attempting to hack the underlying code of the cosmos and building their own synthetic computing capabilities may have been coded into the original software of the cosmos.[8] And the case they make is logically more compelling than the cases for either consciousness being a mere accident or the result of pure divine intervention after the fact of creation.

But regardless of anyone's individual views on this topic, the collective reasoning of the scientific community as a whole has led us to conclude that in the first instant of the formation of the universe—however that instant might most accurately be described—some kind of First Encoding occurred. That original code then immediately started to run, enabling all the other encodings and runtimes that have followed.

■ ■ ■

Framing the universe itself as code may seem a little far-fetched. But it is a framing that is well-grounded in the empirical observations of science and the mathematical logic of theoretical physics. Our conscious everyday experience of the world is that of solid objects, visible light, countless sounds, and fluctuating temperatures. This seemingly tangible world, however, is far less substantial than it appears to us. Visible light is merely our idiosyncratic interpretation of a narrow spectrum of wireless data transmission. Those countless sounds are just a way we decode the movements of our own eardrums. And those temperatures are simply how we perceive the movement of molecules that are themselves comprised of nothings—or at least almost-nothings.

---

[8] See for example *Universe in Creation* by Roy Gould.

We live in a cosmos that was encoded long ago. And that original code continues to run inexorably across a universal computing platform that we are only starting to grasp. Yet all of our experiences, achievements, joys, and pains occur and are enabled by this singular code. We are forever running that code—and that code is forever running us.

PART II:
THE TRANSCENDENT AND THE TANGIBLE

7

To be or to not be: The transcendence of software

Now that we've looked at the basics of software—and how the principles of software apply to the universe beyond computing—it's time to address a critical assertion made at the very beginning of this book: Software does not exist.

It's understandable if you immediately resist this assertion. You've probably downloaded software many times. You may be running several apps right now—and you can see them running on your computer or smartphone. People obviously created those apps, and everyone you know uses them. Surely those downloads and that constant usage are evidence of something that exists.

But here's the thing. When you download software, the software company you get it from doesn't send you any "stuff" to put into your device. That is, you don't actually receive anything tangible we could rightly call "software." Instead, you receive a signal that tells your device how to configure some bits of its memory to replicate the kind of _unitized abstraction_ we examined in Chapter 3. Your device obeys those instructions to create its own _ordered instantiation_ (or "instance") of the software—which it can then invoke as necessary to help you find an all-you-can-eat restaurant in your zipcode or slay some animated zombies with your friends.

Your device only uses the matter and energy already available to it to create its new instance of the software. The computer from which you download the software "talks" to your device over the Internet—but it does not add anything with any discernible existence to your device.

The message your device receives over the Internet from software company's computer when you get some new app is typically not even a bit-for-bit copy of the software itself. Instead, the software company provides your device with a set of instructions on how to create a compressed installation file for the software. Then, when decompressed and opened, that installation file gives your device instructions on how to create a full instance of the software. This file most likely also surveys your device so that the software instance it builds on your computer appropriately takes into account your device's idiosyncrasies—such as its particular version of a given operating system.

Increasingly, software companies don't even tell your device how to create a new instance of an entire application. Instead, software companies only tell your device how to build a relatively small body of code called a "client app." This small client app doesn't have to do all the work of the full app. Instead, it merely has to enable your personal device to communicate over the Internet with some much larger and more complex software running remotely in the cloud, as we saw in Chapter 4.

If software existed in the way we normally think of "existence," software companies would have to make a tangible copy of their code and send it to you. But they don't. In fact, the only empirically detectable change that occurs on your device is a decrease in entropy[9], because the bits on your hard drive become more "ordered" than they were before your device executed its instructions about how to build the software. The energy required for this decrease in entropy,

---

[9] Entropy is technically a measure of energy that cannot be translated into mechanical work. A decrease in entropy on your device basically means that your device's hard drive has become more organized and less random.

however, doesn't come from the software company. It comes from your device's battery—or from the wall socket it's plugged into.

Here's another way to think about this replication without tangible substance. If you want to make lasagna like your Grandma, you don't have to ask her to send you all the physical ingredients. She doesn't even have to send you a physical copy of written instructions. All Grandma has to do is talk. And what she tells you will probably be very "chunked"—because she doesn't have to tell you how to boil water or milk your own cows. Your job is to simply run an _ordered instantiation_ of her recipe. Nothing has to move between the two of you except information.

Code, in other words, is not tangible. It isn't something you can see, feel, or otherwise perceive with your senses. It's not something you can observe with a microscope or a spectrometer. It has no mass and emits no energy. It has none of the attributes of anything that "is" in our usual sense of the word. It's simply a set of abstract values in relationship to each other.

Of course, you could examine your device's drive and see the physical media of that drive arranged in a configuration of 0s and 1s that correspond to a particular application's 0s and 1s. But that's not the software. That's hardware that has been configured to instantiate the software. To claim that you're seeing the software itself is like claiming that a recipe for lasagna —or perhaps that the index card you wrote the recipe on—is edible lasagna.

A map of the world is not the world. Bits of hardware instantiating a software application are not a software application. In fact, no matter how much software we write and how much that software does, software inherently lacks any tangible, empirical existence.

To put it another way, software is not tangible. It is a transcendent phenomenon.

8

To be or to not be: Transcendence everywhere

Let's continue to examine this contrast between that which exists tangibly (specific, concrete instantiations of software) and that which does not (the values-in-relation that is software itself)—and is therefore transcendent.

We can start with language. Right now, you may think that you are in possession of a book (or ebook) called *The Software Revelation*. And, sure, in one sense you are. You have a copy or instance of the book. But that's not the book itself. It's simply a delivery vehicle for an instance of the book in the form of ink on paper or pixels on a screen.

The book itself, however, is something entirely different. *The Software Revelation* is an attempt by one person to communicate some ideas to many other people. I've attempted to convey those ideas using alphanumeric values chunked into words chunked into sentences chunked into paragraphs chunked into chapters. But both my ideas and the sequence of alphanumeric values I've utilized to express those ideas are abstractions that are independent of any particular instantiation of the book. You could change all kinds of attributes of the particular instance of *The Software Revelation* you now possess— the font, the dimensions of the page, the material it's made of—and you'd still have *The Software Revelation*.

Even burning your copy of the book (which you may be tempted to do at this point) wouldn't diminish the work itself in any way. It would only destroy one instantiation of the book. The book is something other than any individual tangible instance of the book.

We can dive deeper into the example of language to consider any individual letter in the book—say, the letter W at the beginning of this paragraph. Is the letter-form W you just saw in print or on your screen the actual letter W? Of course not. It's just an expression of the letter. It's a shape on the page that could be W or W or **W** or *W*. But those various letterforms aren't the letter itself. They are just convenient signifiers of the lexical value W—an intangible value that is quite distinct from any particular instance of a letter on any particular page.

Again, you could burn this book and all the W letterforms in it. The letter W itself would in no way be diminished.

You might even interpret a shape that resembles the letter-form W as the letter W—even though it isn't intended to represent an actual W.[10] That's because your visual processing faculties have been conditioned to interpret that general shape as a letter-form in a language-code you use every day.

The language of mathematics is another useful example to consider—because, despite the fact that it can be applied to countless concrete instantiations ("If you're on a train going 100 miles per hour that's 50 miles behind a train going 85 miles per hour…"), mathematics is in its essence entirely about intangibles.

---

[10] Spoiler alert: An example of an entity that is only accidentally a W is the configuration of palm trees that appears at the end of the 1963 movie "It's a Mad, Mad, Mad, Mad World."

Even a simple assertion such as "1+1=2" is about nothing we could reasonably claim to have any observable existence. There's simply no such thing as "1." "1" doesn't exist anywhere in the universe. Neither do "2," "plus," or "equals." They are signifiers of the intangible. Very powerful and practical intangibles, for sure—but intangibles nonetheless.

Music offers another clear example of the essential "isn't" vs. an instantiated "is." The musical score for Beethoven's Fifth Symphony, for example, isn't the actual symphony. It's simply a set of notations that guide musicians and the conductor as they attempt to perform the symphony at some given time and place. And even when you hear Beethoven's Fifth being performed, the sound waves emanating from the performers' instruments and striking your eardrums aren't the symphony itself. They're a product of one particular performance of the symphony.

The symphony itself, ultimately, is a set of musical values in relationship to each other. Those values and their relationships to each other are not contingent on how some particular conductor has a particular violin section play some sequence of notes on paper during some particular performance. The code of the symphony doesn't exist in space and time at all.

To underscore this notion, consider the fact that I could invoke Beethoven's Fifth just by singing "Dah dah dah DAHH!" I could even sing it horribly off-key. You'd probably be able to interpret the musical reference from that little snippet of my badly executed musical runtime—because Beethoven's opening thematic code is so fault-tolerantly distinctive. The Fifth is a true masterpiece that many of us have been touched by and that has travelled all over the world—yet it doesn't actually exist anywhere. Only ordered (and disordered) instantiations of it do.

Einstein also wrote some masterpieces—in his case, masterpieces of insight into the code of the cosmos. But those masterpieces about code were also code themselves. A hard copy of Einstein's 1905 paper on his theory of special relativity is not his theory of special relativity. His theory is an abstraction that exists nowhere, yet has a specific identity independent of any instantiation thereof.

We could say the same thing about genetic code. Messenger RNA is a long strand of molecules that directs the fabrication of proteins by virtue of its physical shape and bio-electrical properties. It thereby enables the material expression of a living being's genetic code. But it's not the code itself. That code is the series of values in relational sequence that exists independently of any particular RNA or DNA strand.

This distinction between genetic code itself and some particular chemical instance of that code is especially evident in genetic engineering. Genetic engineers first decide how to change an amino acid sequence based on the proteins they want to have synthesized in the genetically modified organism (GMO) they're engineering. It's only *after* they make that decision about code in the abstract that they then concretely instantiate the code by engineering it in molecular form. Engineered code that has not already occurred in nature must first be conceived as an abstraction in the mind of an engineer— just as his Fifth Symphony first occurred only as an unobservable, immaterial abstraction in Beethoven's mind.

And genetic code isn't the only kind of "natural" code we can engineer. Using the principles of Mendeleev's unitized abstraction of the elements, we've been able to predict elements that we hadn't yet discovered and even synthesize new ones never seen in nature. Here again—in the building blocks of the tangible universe—we can see that the underlying code itself is an abstraction. Only in its concrete instantiations does that code manifest as tangible "stuff."

Software, in other words, doesn't have any tangible, empirical existence—whether that software was written by humans or written by nature long before humans came along.[11]

We may therefore be justified in asserting that the cosmos itself is inherently transcendent. And if this is the case, then its transcendence is certainly worth exploring further.

---

[11] Readers who are familiar with the history of philosophy should be careful not to confuse this distinction between transcendent code and tangible iteration with Platonism or Neo-Platonism. To assert that Beethoven's Fifth can't be fully located in a given instance of the Fifth is not Platonic—because it is not an assertion that Beethoven was the vehicle for manifesting some musical or esthetic ideal. The Fifth is just Beethoven being Beethoven.

9

Qualia and the software of consciousness

Software isn't just a useful model for understanding language, music, cooking, biology, and the physics of the universe. It's also a useful model for understanding our own consciousness—i.e., the very means by which we engage with language, music, cooking, biology, and the physics of the universe.

In fact, we may be able to argue that human consciousness is essentially the software we run on the hardware of our brains, rather than something directly emergent from our brain hardware itself.

The example of color perception can help us build an argument for this model. When you see red, you're interpreting a certain wavelength of light as "red." But the light isn't red *per se*. It is instead a wave with a length of somewhere between 625 and 740 nanometers. Our human visual apparatus, however, has evolved to decode the subjective experience of light within that frequency range as "redness."[12]

"Redness," in other words, is a kind of convenient decoding for light wavelengths within a certain portion of the visible spectrum. No one says, "My favorite dress reflects ambient light at a wavelength of 713

---

[12] Some people, of course, are colorblind. Others are able to discern subtle differences in color that escape the rest of us. These differences in color perception don't change the fact every time someone sees a particular quality of light, corresponding qualia occur in their consciousness.

nm." We say "I love my red dress"—even though that dress wouldn't look red in a blue light.[13]

Also, we all have our own personal semiotic associations with the color red. That is, red may convey meanings to us aside from its basic function as a way to decode a given wavelength of light. At a traffic light, red means stop. On a balance sheet, red means a loss. Red can also invoke anger or the logo of a local sports team. These meanings have been encoded into red differently for every individual—and we decode them without a second thought.

More to the point, your personal, subjective experience of "redness" is an example of something we can technically refer to as "qualia" (or "quale" in the singular). "Qualia" is a great word, because it gives a name to something that's very real—for example, your subjective experience of the "redness" of an object—but that has no empirically observable being.

Let's be clear about how totally intangible our qualia—our subjective conscious experiences of the world—are. Even if advances in physical brain science eventually enable us to determine exactly how light stimulates our retinas and sets off the impulses that stimulate our brains to experience "red" and all of its semiotic associations, we will still only be describing a set of phenomena in hardware. What you directly and personally experience when you see red—the "redness" that occurs in your conscious mind—is still something apart from the physical stimuli that trigger your perception of color.

Qualia are your real experiences, but they have no empirically verifiable existence. They are fleeting phenomena of the software

---

[13] FWIW, your brain can also be fooled into seeing "red" by messing with your optical hardware. See, for example, the classic optical illusion of staring at an image of the American flag in green, yellow, and black—then looking at a white wall, where an afterimage of red, white, and blue appears.

running in your mind. They cannot be directly and objectively observed by any other person or any scientific instrument.

Color perception is just one example of qualia. What you experience when you hear a sound, what you sense when you smell a certain aroma, how you process your feelings of love or disgust, what happens inside your being as you process pain or parenthood—these are all real facts of consciousness, even though they have no empirically observable existence. In fact, *by definition* they cannot exist anywhere but your own consciousness.

The reality of qualia is critical to our understanding of ourselves and our world. Some people like to say that "Facts don't care about your feelings." But, like it or not, feelings are themselves a type of fact. They are genuine facts of consciousness. My sadness about the fact that I only have $50 in my bank account is no less a reality than the fact that I only have $50 in my checking account. Of course, my $50 balance can be accurately and empirically measured—while my sadness is a subjective experience that cannot. This difference in empirical observability, however, doesn't change the reality that both my bank balance and my experience of my bank balance are facts in the same cosmos.

Because these paired realities occur at the same time in the same cosmos—and because they are causally linked to each other—it's clearly sensible to suggest that we apply the same rational framework to both. Transcendent phenomena such as qualia (i.e. our direct subjective experience of consciousness) and the tangible, empirical world of physics, chemistry, biology, and the like are certainly *distinguishable* from each other—but they do not inhabit two entirely distinct realms. To continue treating them as if they do is to complacently languish in an obsolete dualism that the study of software empowers us to falsify.

We'll look more at dualism later, but for now let's just say that our everyday metaphysical schizophrenia is logically and philosophically problematic. It just doesn't make much sense to use one set of conceptual tools to describe the cosmos and another to describe our experience of that same cosmos. After all, we are obviously part of the cosmos; we are not outside or separate from it. To exempt our own direct experience of consciousness from our conceptual framework of the universe is a kind of intellectual cheating that doesn't stand up to truly diligent rational scrutiny.

■ ■ ■

We've now reached the end of Section II. Thus far, we've examined the nature of software and seen how software reveals the pervasiveness of transcendence in a universe we might otherwise view as entirely tangible. In Section III, we'll focus on one particular aspect of software—relationality—to better understand transcendence. What software reveals to us about relationality will, in fact, be critical to our successful escape from the fallacy of dualism as we embrace a far more coherent, unified, and practical worldview.

PART III:
RELATIONALITY

(a/k/a THE SPACES BETWEEN STUFF)

10

The primacy of relations

At the beginning of this book, I asked you to at least temporarily accept a definition of software as "values in relationship to each other." I made the case that this was a good working definition because software in its most conventional form is a series of 0s and 1s (i.e., two basic binary _values_) in a precisely ordered sequence (i.e., well-defined _relationships to each other_).

We then saw how this definition of software can be extended to other phenomena where the _values_ are not binary and the _relationships_ are not necessarily linear sequence. The coding of Western music, for example, uses the twelve _values_ of the chromatic scale—and _relationships_ between notes that include rhythmic time and relative volume, as well as sequence.

If you take a moment to thoughtfully consider how I wrote this definition of software—and how you read it—you may notice that both you and I may unconsciously tend to emphasize the _values_ in our definition over their _relationships_. That is, we have an innate tendency to think of _values_ as the main element in the software equation, while the _relationships_ between them are a sort secondary attribute associated with those values.[14]

---

[14] Those of you familiar with deconstruction may choose to think of this emphasis as a hierarchical "privileging" of values over relationships between values.

This unconscious prejudice may be in part because the _values_ in our software-based models are more plainly apparent to us, while their _relationships_ to each other are relatively opaque. We can easily see the 0s and 1s in a written depiction of binary code, but nothing about their order immediately or obviously jumps out at us. Some of us may easily recognize the pattern in a structurally ordered sequence of digits such as 001001001 or 1011011101111011111. But we'll probably perceive a sequence like 01001011011101000001010111 to be completely random—even though it represents a highly ordered and specific set of instructions to a certain kind of computer.

Similarly, while it is obvious to you that this page is filled with letterforms, their relationship to each other tends to disappear into our automatic reading of words and sentences. You probably don't even read the word "word" as a 'w' followed by an "o" followed by an "r" followed by a "d"—but instead just chunk it as a complete word.

Music offers another example of how our understanding of "values in relationship to each other" can unconsciously see to be about _values_ first and _relationships_ second. We readily perceive the individual sound-values in a piece of music: there's the three notes of a memorable opening guitar lick, there's the singer coming in with a single long note requiring amazing lung power. We may not, however, take fully conscious notice of the relationship between those notes (i.e. that the first two notes of the guitar lick are timed close together and are only a small interval apart, while the third is delayed by a beat-and-a-half and jumps up an entire octave).

This values-over-relationship prejudice is commonplace. We look up at the night sky and easily see the stars, but may only become conscious of their relative positions after we learn about the constellations they comprise. We see five cows in a field, but don't consider their spatial relationship to each other unless there is something exceptionally noticeable about it—like them being in a perfect circle or straight line.[15]

Turning back to computer software for a moment, let's again consider the relationship of values to each other in the code-snippet 010010110111010000101010111. How can we understand and describe that set of relationships? It's certainly not easy to do so. In fact, it may be impossible to adequately describe what's going on relationally in even such a small snippet of code without deep technical knowledge about programming. You probably didn't even notice that it's the exact same sequence of 0s and 1s I used a few paragraphs earlier.

Describing the relationship between values in a genetic codon sequence of three amino acids may be a bit easier for us—but the same principle still applies. We can readily see and describe the relational difference between "CGC" and "CCG." Both contain two cytosine values and one guanine value. The sequential relationship between the last two values, however, is transposed in the second codon.

Without any expertise in genetics, though, this difference in sequential relationship will be absolutely meaningless to us—just as someone who doesn't understand English would be unable to comprehend the semantic difference between "page" and "gape."

Put another way, in both the examples of genetics and language above, we much more readily zero in on and recognize simple individual values than we do the highly complex relationships among values.

We need to pay very close attention to this tendency we have to more readily perceive the _values_ in software-based models and to give them a kind of existential primacy over the _relationships_ of those values to each other. We know what 0s and 1s are. Relationships between 0s and 1s, on the other hand, are far less familiar and tangible to us.

---

[15] Again, for deconstruction fans, we might relate this prejudice to the privileging of _presence_ over _absence_.

This is a crucial point in our investigation of what the title of this book refers to as the "software revelation," because I am about to argue that we need to entirely flip this innate cognitive prejudice on its head. And this argument will require active mental effort on your part to at least temporarily **give the _relationships_ between values primacy over the _values_ themselves**—despite the way our minds seem to innately do just the opposite.

This reversal of primacy is absolutely central to our process of discovery—and to everything that follows in this book—so I encourage you to not take it lightly. We will see later why _relationships_ are so central to the software-inspired re-thinking of our metaphysics (or, perhaps better yet, our phenomenology) as a whole. But let's first consider why this radical shift in emphasis—which I'd like to term _"relational primacy"_—makes sense.

Software and sequence

Every instance of software is uniquely itself solely because of the _relationships_ between the values in its code, not the _values_ themselves. This is patently obvious because all apps have the same value units: 0s and 1s. Nothing about any individual 0 or 1 is distinctive. They are simply tools that enable encoding and decoding by electronic hardware that operates on the principle of "on" (1) and "off" (0). What makes your favorite apps your favorite apps are the _relationships_ between their 0s and 1s—not the 0s and 1s themselves.

Values don't really play any role at all in the distinctive functionality of an app. The 37,045th 0 or 1 in an application doesn't have any inherent, independent meaning (just as it lacks any inherent, independent existence). That 37,045th 0 or 1 only means what it means and does what it does because it immediately follows the 37,044[th] 0 or 1 in the code, which in turn follows the other 37,043 0s and 1s.

In other words, a binary digit only has meaning—and thereby the associated ability to cause something to happen (i.e., agency)—by virtue of its relationship to other binary digits. Or, put still another way, **a value's agency is entirely contingent on its relational context.**

Drop a 0 here or add a 1 there, and the agency of every following digit will be changed or nullified. The result might just be a weirdly out-of-place pixel on your screen. Or it could be a so-called "fatal" error that causes the entire application to crash. But the relationships of values in software are essential. Screwing up any of those relationships screws up your code.

This doesn't mean that software has zero tolerance for relational error. As we noted earlier, software and hardware have lots of mechanisms to detect potential errors in code and to automatically correct those errors if possible. Those mechanisms, however, only underscore the importance of _relationships_ between values in sequence—because that's exactly what they check.

We'll see later how this principle of _relational primacy_ relates to all our other examples of software-like phenomena. But for the moment, let's agree that generally speaking we can extend what we learn about computer software to other phenomena that fit our software model of values-in-relationship.

Now let's combine the principle of _relational primacy_—i.e., that any particular piece of software is what it is and can do what it does primarily because of the _relationships_ that exist between its constituent values—with the second of the two foundational truths we started with: that software doesn't exist empirically (i.e., it is transcendent, rather than tangible).

Together, I believe *relational primacy* and the reality of software's *transcendence* lead us logically to a centrally important conclusion:

> ***Transcendent phenomena are endowed with their***
> ***identity and agency by relationality.[16]***

Yes, all the transcendent software-analogous phenomena we've examined thus far are built on some kind of *values*. But those values, as we saw in Chapters 3 and 4, are simply mechanisms for abstraction and instantiation. Ultimately, it's the *relationships* between values that make any given piece of transcendent software what it is, that distinguish it from any other piece of software, and that endow it with its particular agency.

This may seem like a somewhat trivial truth about software. But as we examine it further, this principle of *relational primacy* will turn out to be quite radical—and central to the claim made in this book's title of a "software revelation."

---

[16] I'm using the term "relationality" here to refer to the state of all the relationships connected with any given value or entity at any given time. In the case of a 0 or 1 in an app, that relationality may consist of nothing more than its sequence in a line of program code. In the case of a town in France, on the other hand, that relationality would be much more complex—including its department, its region, its proximity to geographic features such as a river or mountain, its natural resources, its agricultural and industrial productivity, its political history, its neighboring towns and cities, etc.

Other examples of "relationality" include the Earth being the third planet from the Sun, Eric Clapton and Jimmy Page having been bandmates in The Byrds, and you now being someone who has read at least a portion of a book I wrote.

"Relationality" is only tangentially related to "relativity," which has more to do with frames of reference than relationships between entities—although I suppose you could say that my relationship to my frame of reference is one piece of my total relationality. I'll further explain what I like about the term "relationality" in Chapter 12.

11

Relationality, identity, and agency

Let's extend our investigation of relationality outward from computer code to the universe as a whole—starting with the example of language. Better yet, let's start with the English word "language" itself.

The word "language" encodes a rich set of meanings that can include the languages we speak and write, the languages we use to write computer software, and other forms of coded communications such as courtship behaviors (the "language of love") and movie directing (the "language of cinema").

The "e" at the end of the word "language" doesn't have any independent semantic meaning—nor is it pronounced in the spoken word. But it conforms to the convention of the English suffix "-age," which helps give the word its noun-ness. Some of us may recognize the root "lang-" in the word, which is a Latinate root for "tongue." That's how the word "language" became English code for so many kinds of verbal and non-verbal software.

If I disturb the relationship between the letters in "language"—and instead write "languag" or "langauge"—you'll probably still understand what I mean. Fortunately, I have a spell-check program that prevents me from making such mistakes as I code my thoughts into modern written English. You also have lots of context clues for properly interpreting those misspellings, because you're reading the word in the context of sentences and paragraphs that obviously refer to "language." So there are lots of error-correcting mechanisms at play as you "run" my code.

Those error-correcting mechanisms might not work as well if you saw the letters out of sequence *and* out of context. They also might not work that well if I made a more serious relationality error like "alanguge"—even though it only has one value out of sequence. "Eanuglga" would probably be completely indecipherable to you—despite the fact that all the letter-values are there—unless I specifically asked you to run the word-unscrambling software in your mind using pen and paper.

I can also have some semantic fun by changing one letter of the word to make it "lunguage." You've never seen this word before, so you have a few choices about how to "run" this strange new bit of code. You can read it as a typo and change it to "language." You could also try to decode it to see if you can extract from it some new, modified meaning. If you know me well enough and the context is right, you might even recognize it as a freshly coined word for "the way we communicate through sighs, moans, and other wordless breaths"—which is symptomatic of my own idiosyncratic and possibly pathological compulsion to pun.

Other codes, other relations

In the case of genetic code, we can similarly see that meaning and efficacy are the property of relationships between amino acids in sequence, rather than in the individual amino acids—or even individual codons—themselves.

Sure, there are actual physical amino acids that in a given sequence physically guide the production of certain proteins—which, in turn, enable various biological capabilities. And, sure, those physical processes can fail in tangible ways if a strand of genetical material is physically broken or altered.

But mutations occur because there is an anomaly in the sequential _relationships_ between amino acids (i.e. the code's relational sequence). If a physical defect in a strand prevents any code from being formed at all, no mutation occurs. Incoherent biochemical "noise" isn't a big problem in reproduction, either. Legitimate values out of proper relationship, on the other hand, are.

And while your genetic code alone by no means fully determines who you are, each of us would be a very different person if our genetic code were altered. With a slight change in my genetic code (plus some luck and a lot of hard work) I might have been a power forward in the NBA. Another slight alteration, and I would have been initially seen as my parents' biological daughter instead of their biological son.

But, again, while my genetics are not wholly determinative of my identity, that identity—and, by extension, my personal agency in the world—is significantly affected by the relationality of my amino acid values. Those acid values themselves are the same for you and me: C, G, A, and T. However, the order of my particular Cs, Gs, As, and Ts contribute to the fact that I wrote this book instead of collecting millions for promoting a sneaker with my name on it.

We can see the principle of _relational primacy_ in music, too. Music isn't just notes. The last DAH in the opening phrase of Beethoven's Fifth only does what it does because of how it follows the preceding dah-dah-dah. "DAH dah-dah-dah" wouldn't even be recognizable to most of us as a transposition of that phrase. The same is true of a Miles Davis trumpet solo. Play the notes of any given Miles solo in some rigid sequence or without the right relative emphasis, and it will be entirely devoid of it Milesishness—and, by extension, all of its transfixing beauty. The expressiveness and artistry of music arise from nuances in the relationality between notes and between the chunks of notes we call "phrases." As Claude Debussy is said to have put it, "Music is the space between the notes."

A corollary to Debussy's assertion about music is Matisse's about his own approach to visual art. "I don't paint things," he said. "I only paint the difference between things."

This principle—that _relationships_ between values have an agency and significance which _values_ themselves utterly lack—is central to the ideas we'll explore in the following chapters. Every piece of software, every piece of music, every person, and every element in the periodic table is what it is and does what it does because of its unique relationality, even though those relationalities are transcendent rather than tangible. Relationality is, in fact, central to any coherent understanding of the transcendent.

12

Three attributes of relationality

The notion that there is something essentially relational about the universe is an ancient one. Many spiritual, religious, and philosophical disciplines throughout history have featured assertions about the "connectedness" of everything. Many wise people over the centuries have also asserted that this inter-relatedness leads inexorably to the conclusion that the entire universe forms some kind of single cosmic "whole."

Rather than borrow ideas about universal connectedness from any particular spiritual, religious, or philosophical tradition, however, I would like us to continue examining the concept of relationality from our own present-day perspective, applying basic reason to the material we've covered thus far concerning the nature of software—whether that software is computer code or any of the other forms of code we've explored.

More specifically, I'd like to suggest that we consider the following three key attributes of relationality:

Attribute 1: Relationality has specificity

One issue I have with many traditional teachings on "connectedness"—teachings that are obviously not informed by the full richness of present-day human knowledge—is that they can get a bit fuzzy about the nature of relationality. Vague assertions about "connectedness" don't define any useful specifics about the nature of the connection between two particular entities—say, between me and you. I'm just somehow supposed to accept that there is some kind of connection between us because somebody told me so.

But if what gives entities their unique agency and identity is their unique relationality, then we should fully acknowledge that uniqueness. After all, the relationship between you and me is quite different from the relationship between me and my older son—which is, in turn, qualitatively different from the relationship between me and my younger son. And none of these relationships are static. They change constantly in both subtle and unsubtle ways over time.

Relationality in the software of music offers us another example of this discoverable specificity. The relationship between two notes a major third apart is quite different from the relationship between two notes a minor third apart—even though that difference is only a half-step, the smallest standard distinction in Western music.

Likewise, a change in the order of just a single amino acid in a codon can have significant consequences for an organism's attributes. And moving just one Jenga block the wrong way in relationship to the other blocks can bring the whole tower down.

By using terms like "relationality" and "relationship"—rather than the vaguer and more generalized notion of universal "connectedness"—we can perhaps strengthen our sense that values and entities of all sorts are associated with each other in highly specific ways. So in addition to better understanding the importance of relationality *generally*, we can also better understand the vital particulars that characterize relationships *specifically*.

Attribute 2: Relationality implies agency

A second issue I have with a generalized notion of "connectedness" is an implicit suggestion that relationships *are*, but don't actually *do*. That is, a mere acknowledgement that there exists some vague connectedness between Entity A and Entity B doesn't tell me anything about how that connectedness engenders any real agency in the world or specifically shapes the identities of the entities involved.

This seems to me to be another obvious error. The most powerful forces in the universe—amongst which I would include gravity and love—are both 1) essentially relational and 2) capable of tremendous agency. Gravity is not merely some abstract connection between me and the planet on which I reside. It is a highly specific relationship that gives my body a very specific weight on Earth and affects my every movement. It can also potentially result in the super-messy splattering of me (and not the Earth) if I fall from a particular height onto a particular surface.

Similarly, the love between me and those closest to me isn't just some vague connectedness. That relationality has very specific and powerful agency. It affects my actions, thoughts, and perhaps even my lifespan. It affects perfect strangers who see us casually expressing our love in public displays of affection. It makes me very happy—and it also sometimes makes me a little crazy.

Team sports are another great example of specificity in relationships. Teams in good relationships accomplish things that their individual members alone could not. And teams with bad relationships can lose despite the talents of their individual members. But these relationships are very different from team to team. Some teams revolve around a single superstar. Others are built on a more distributed set of responsibilities. Relationships thus not only each have their own specific qualities—they also engender their own specific agencies.

Attribute 3: Relationality is complexly tiered

Thirdly, vague assertions about universal connectedness gloss over the hierarchical complexity of relationality. Relationships have relationships with other relationships. And those relationships have higher-order relationships with each other. To merely posit that "everything is connected" is to minimize the multi-faceted chunking that is so central to the nature of our encoded universe and the way we operate within it.

Software components in our digital systems constantly interact with each other. The app running on your phone may be comprised of one functional unit of code that manages the interface, another that handles data for your active session, and still another that manages communications with back-end software running on the app's cloud servers.

This modular software architecture empowers developers to freely mix-and-match functional units of code to create new digital capabilities without having to re-write every subfunction from scratch. Modular architecture also enables developers to rapidly make changes in one discrete functional unit of an app without running the risk of making a mistake that screws up the entire app from top to bottom.

Developers thus constantly engineer relationality between chunks of code that are themselves sets of relationships between bits. Those multi-modular applications, in turn enter into digital relationships with other multi-modular applications. It is because of this tiered modularity that banks are able to quickly adopt new payment systems and online retailers can adaptively aggregate inventory data from third-party suppliers.

This complex, multi-tiered relationality is evident everywhere. Both the Moon and I, for example, have gravitational relationships with the Earth—which is in a rather significant gravitational relationship with the Sun. My relationship with my mother and father was affected by their relationship with each other. My relationship with my parents then affected my relationships with my own children—whose relationships with each other and with me, in turn, affected their relationship with their grandparents.

More to the point, I am not just in relationships with my loved ones, the planet, and the universe as a whole. I have a diversity of relationships that include family, community, business, culture, and politics—which are themselves contingent on relationships that other family members, citizens, etc. have with each other. I have neighbors I see often, but with whom I interact only superficially. On the other hand, there are people I've never met in person with whom I've communicated with online pretty intensively for years—because we're part of larger social networks that intersect in very specific ways.

I have strong ties to my own hometown because of all the experiences I had there and all the relationships that developed there. I have another strong tie to my paternal grandfather's hometown because of its connection to a complex network of family relationships and a tragic national history. I also have an oddly strong tie to a road that leads north from Brescia through the fields of Lombardy because of the way the sun was shining there one special evening when I'd run out of money after having spent my last few lira on a cab ride back to the train station. All this relationality is deeply fascinating in its diverse connections, hierarchies of connections, specificities and cascading effects.

Networks of relationality are rich with meaning and agency because every person, place, and thing with which we connect in some special way is itself connected to other people, places, and things in their own special ways.

In fact, the mathematical reality is that ***there are many, many more relationships between things than there are things***. A vague notion of some universal "connectedness" does not fully reflect this complex, pervasive, and highly specific relational reality. Conversely, a much more substantive concept of relationality seems necessary as we attempt to come to terms with *relational primacy*.

13

The relationality of stuff

Back in Chapter 10, I asked you to take what I consider to be the very crucial and challenging step of giving _relationships_ primacy over the _values_ or entities in those relationships. I asked you to do this because it is my contention that _the identity and agency of transcendent phenomena arise from relationality._

In Chapter 11, I sought to support that claim by having us examine the importance of relationality in language and other types of software.

Then, in Chapter 12, we made a clear distinction between some vague, general sense of universal "connectedness" and the highly specific relationality between values, entities, people, and even relationships themselves. I closed that chapter with a simple observation that I believe further supports this notion of _relational primacy_—namely, that **there are many, many more relationships between things than there are things.**

In this chapter, we will stay focused on _relational primacy_ by considering whether we can reasonably such a principle to the very stuff of the cosmos.

Put another way, I'm going to ask you to see the universe as a multitude of transcendent relationships that can at times manifest tangibly—rather than as a multitude of tangible things that just happen to interact with each other in some general way.

Again, I'm hoping you don't minimize either the importance or the intellectual difficulty of this challenge. If we're successful, we will basically turn our world-view upside down—elevating relationality from a secondary (or, in more philosophically technical terms, "accidental") attribute of entities to a primary (or "essential") one.

Ultimately, we may even come close to eliminating non-relational attributes from our understanding of the cosmos entirely. But for now, let's just try to see that relationality is what makes things what they are and what enables them to do what they do.

This isn't easy. In our everyday lives, we experience the world as tangible things: a table, a chair, trees, cars, food, physical human beings. But, as we'll consider later, this entity-centric view of the world may just be a practical way to "chunk" the infinitely complex relationality of the cosmos we live in. If we try, we may be able to peel away that chunked layer of perceived tangibility to arrive at a compelling and quite useful underlying truth about transcendence.

Rock and role

Let's start with a simple thought-experiment. When you look down and see a rock, it's pretty natural to think to yourself "That's a rock." And you're not wrong.

But that rock you're seeing isn't what it is independently of everything else. For one thing, it's the particular rock you're seeing and being conscious of through your sense of sight at that particular moment. It's the only rock that exists at a very particular location in space at a very particular time—which is why you happen to see it at that moment. And the only reason you're seeing it the way you're seeing it is because of how it's reflecting the light striking it at that specific time and place.

That rock came from somewhere and is heading somewhere else. That is, it is relational to an origin and a destination. If you had sufficient knowledge of geology, you might understand that rock as evidence of some eons-long rock origination story. And if you had sufficient knowledge of local history, you might also know how it wound up being right there in front of you at the very moment you happened to be passing by.

Physics has even more to say about the relationality of the rock. As solid and stationary as the rock may appear, we know that there's lots of motion and energy bouncing around throughout the rock—and that the rock is mostly empty space. The rock's composition is being determined at this very moment by all kinds of tiny subparticles whirring and spinning around each other. Despite appearances at the level of human sight, the rock is busier than a postal sorting facility before Christmas.

Quantum theory even tells us that if you were to try to observe the rock at a subatomic level, the rock would present itself in different ways—as either particles or waves—depending on how you, the observer, chose to observe it. That is, even as a mere observer of the rock, you have been put into a non-trivial relationship with its very being.

If you change your relationship with the rock, you change the rock itself. Kick it, and you change something fundamental about its identity: instead of being the rock that's right here, it becomes the rock that used to be right there—but that's now all the way over there.

Break the rock. Are there now two rocks? Did the original rock cease to exist? You didn't zap it out of existence—so maybe you now have two pieces of one rock that are not whole rocks themselves. Or do you?

And while you're doing this, you've been changed too. You have become The Kicker and Breaker of One Unfortunate Rock. That's not who you were before. And if you try to smash the rock with your foot, you may injure yourself and wind up with a scar—in which case you will be marked by the rock forever.[17]

The point of this thought-experiment is not to nonsensically over-complicate the simple act of seeing a rock. The point is to highlight the reality that just about everything that makes that rock "that rock" is relational. And when those relations are changed, the rock is no longer what it was—but becomes something else. And so do we.

Does this mean we have to acquire accurate knowledge of all the specific relational attributes of every rock we encounter so that we don't mistakenly think of it as just some rock? Of course not. In fact, in an upcoming chapter, we will take a look at how we use narrative overlays to functionally streamline (or chunk) our engagement with a universe that is absolutely saturated with relational complexities far beyond our comprehension.

But the simple example of a rock is a good starting point for considering the possibility that, while it may be functionally advantageous for us to chunk our perception of the things we encounter every day as tangible, discrete entities unto themselves, those things may not be discrete entities at all—but are instead first and foremost a nexus of relationships at a particular time and place.

---

[17] I put the short poem "Anecdote of the Jar" by Wallace Stevens at the beginning of this book precisely because I think it does a fantastic job of expressing this notion of things being in relationship to their environments.

14

More about the relationality of stuff

This principle of _relational primacy_—i.e., that an entity's relationality is what defines its identity and gives it its agency—is worth exploring further with other examples. Let's consider a table for our next case. What makes a table a table? And what makes a particular table _that_ particular table?

One definition of "table" in my Webster's New World Dictionary is "a piece of furniture consisting of a flat top set horizontally on legs." This is, of course, only one definition. The world "table" can also refer to data arranged in rows and columns, a flat surface cut on top of a diamond or other precious stone, etc. But you knew from context which kind of table I meant.

It's worth noting that Webster's definition of "table" describes a _relationship_ between a flat surface and the legs that support it. But we can quickly see that a table's legs only become a table's legs when they support a surface.

Our understanding of things often bounces back and forth across a relationship like this in both directions. When I was in college, I didn't have money for a proper coffee table, so I just laid my electric piano's hard case on top of my two stereo speakers. The result was certainly a "table" of sorts, but only because the relation between my speakers and my piano case turned them into "table legs" and a "tabletop," respectively.

There are also tables that don't really have legs at all because they're more like boxes. Are the sides of these boxy tables their "legs?" Do such tables make the Webster's definition problematic? Are such tables really cabinets masquerading as tables?

And what makes a coffee table a coffee table—as opposed to, say, a dining room table? Clearly, the identities of such tables are based on their physical characteristics. But we identify those physical characteristics based on the relationship between such tables and their users. Dining room tables relate to our bodies' proportions in such a way that they are more comfortable for consuming full meals while facing each other. Coffee tables are lower and take up less floor space in rooms where we are more likely to serve snacks than full meals—and where we may want to move around more easily or watch something on TV.

And if a book relates to the dimensions and function of a coffee table in the appropriate way, it becomes more than just a book. It becomes a *coffee table* book!

Building codes

Next, let's consider buildings. We can again use a dictionary definition of "building"—or just rely on our own sense that a building is any kind of somewhat permanent man-made structure.

But while that may be a useful definition of what we classify as a "building" generally, we really don't relate to individual structures that way at all. Your home is a building—but it's a very specific building with very specific relational attributes for you and your family. You may not even call it a building. You probably all it your home, your apartment, your condo, or your castle.

Many people don't have a place to call "home." This homelessness (i.e. null relationality with a building that could be functionally and personally identifiable as their "home") radically affects their identity and their social relations.

I grew up in the same single-family home for my entire childhood and adolescence. Every time I re-visit that particular building, it evokes a multitude of memories and feelings. If you entered that same building, I doubt you'd have even a fleeting thought about a Mahler symphony on the record player or a shrine to the Apollo moon mission that a nerdy kid once created in the small closet under the basement stairs. But I do.

Buildings also have very strong relationships to their locations and histories. A building's materials are often related to its local environment: lumber where wood is readily available, earthen materials such as rock and clay where it's not. The forms of buildings can be driven by environmental factors too: steep roofs where heavy snow falls, open airflow in hot climates. The design of a structure built in the late 1700's is quite different from that of one built in the early 2000's.

And, of course, we tend to identify buildings by how they relate to the community functionally. A bank is a building where money matters are managed. Banks have thus historically acquired an atmosphere of security and stability. Lots of financial transactions take place at casinos as well. But those transactions are of a very different nature, so a casino's physical attributes are quite different from a bank's— right down to the patterns on the rug and the sounds that fill the air.

■ ■ ■

We could look at lots of entities in this same manner: cars, clothes, computers, cats, companies, countries, and more. The key concept here is that there doesn't seem to be any real "table" at the heart of a table or any real "country" at the heart of a "country." Things are only what they are because of how everything relates to them and how they relate to everything else. We call a rock a rock and an airplane an airplane—but each entity is uniquely itself only because of the complex internal and external relationality occurring at a given time and place. This rational, scientifically supportable understanding of the cosmos leads us inexorably to the principle of *relational primacy*.

15

How relational are we?

Now let's examine our own personal being in this same light of relationality and _relational primacy_. I'll take the liberty of supposing that most of us have an innate sense of ourselves as discrete beings with our own unique nature apart from any relationships that we may have. Sure, we may have siblings, friends, and bosses, but in our everyday experience of ourselves, we frame our existence as consisting of some "real self"—an inner core of our being that perceives, thinks, feels, and acts in ways that we don't always manifest in our presentation of ourselves to the outside world.

That framing is useful. To function in society, we need to have a sense of self. I have my own private PIN number for my ATM card—and when I withdraw my cash, I don't just hand it over to strangers (unless, of course, I'm in a mood). I look for my own car in the parking lot when I'm ready to go home, because that's the one I can start with the key in my pocket. And I definitely don't share my Social Security number with anyone if I can avoid it.

But I'm also going to assert that even this individual being that I impute to myself is profoundly relational, rather than fully independent and discrete.

I personally experience the world as I do because I was born in a particular place and time, because the genetics I inherited from my birth-parents create certain biochemical predispositions when it comes to emotion and sensation, because things people have done to me or said to me are deeply imprinted on my consciousness. I am constantly being conditioned by the responses to my actions and behaviors reflected back to me in the world—responses which generate feedback unique to my particular culture, geography, social identity, and biology.

Change my relationships, and you change me. Many of us can attest to how our sense of ourselves was affected by a relationship with an abusive spouse or a great friend. Our relationships with finances, drugs, or a hobby can alter our being as well. Some of us even become a very different person simply by listening to the right song or experiencing the sights, sounds, and scents of the sea.

Much of our sense of ourselves as discrete, tangible beings comes from the fact that we live within our own skin, that we have our own names, and that we are treated by others as being not-them. But we should be careful about taking these outward characteristics as indicators of incontrovertible truth.[18]

For one thing, science tells us that our physical bodies are much less solid and stable than they appear to be. We noted earlier how a rock, according to physics, is a dance of subatomic particles and forces—so it's much more "nothing" than it is "something." The same obviously goes for us. And from a biological perspective, the cells in our bodies are constantly dying and regenerating—so materially we're hardly the same "we" that we were just a little while ago.

Plus, we have all sorts of strange flora living inside our guts, helping us digest the food that becomes part of our bodies every day. We're constantly passing air, water, and food from the outside world through

---

[18] There is an extended passage near the end of Chapter Ten in Thomas Mann's Confessions of Felix Krull where Krull directly addresses the issue of "living separately and divided from others inside [our] own skin." It's too long to quote here in full—but I recommend it for its relevance to the subject of this chapter.

our organs. Even the skin that seems to define the border of "me" is pretty porous. So the claim that we're solid, discrete entities is scientifically pretty iffy.

This fluid relationality doesn't mean that we must necessarily deny our individual existence altogether. Perhaps at the nexus of all these relationships with people, places, and things there is in fact some central point of being—an "I" that is the common endpoint of these seemingly infinite radiating lines of relationality.

But that "I" may be much less substantive and much less innately itself than we think it is. "Self" could instead be some almost-nothing thing which exists solely to relate to other entities (which are themselves purely or almost purely relational)—rather than some rich repository of innate properties belonging to some independent, fully-formed being.

Religious traditions offer different ways of understanding this tiny shred of almost-nothing we call the "self." Much of the Western tradition posits a "spirit" or "soul" at the core of our individual being. Hindu tradition also posits an *atman* (a Sanskrit word that we could translate as "soul") capable of being reincarnated.

Buddhism, on the other hand, departs from traditional Hinduism by asserting the doctrine of *anatman* (or "no-soul"). According to this teaching, the individual being is composed of five "aggregates" (loosely translatable as matter, sensation, perception, mental formations, and consciousness). Putting together these aggregates to make a "self" is somewhat akin to making a table out of speakers and a piano case. Calling such constructions a "self" or a "table" may be convenient and even accurate in some way—but they're really just temporary amalgamations of elements in relationship with each other, rather than truly discrete independent entities.

We don't have to take a strong position one way or the other on the soul/no-soul question. Indeed, we may not have all the information and/or reasoning capabilities we need to reach a strong conclusion about our own selves. But whether everything I am is entirely endowed to me by relationality alone (*anatman*) or there is some inner point of being that makes me me (*atman*), it is clear that we are not merely connected to the cosmos in some vague "spiritual" way. *We are profoundly relational beings in a profoundly relational cosmos.*

And, while on a day-to-day basis it may be convenient for us to see ourselves as independently functioning hardware, we—like the rest of the universe—seem to have much more in common with software.

The next item on our agenda should therefore perhaps be to look more closely at how it is that transcendent, relational beings such as ourselves manage to functionally navigate our way through a transcendent, relational cosmos. How and why do we manage to see the transcendent as tangible? And can the methods of consciousness that cause us to see the transcendent as tangible also somehow be used to see the tangible as transcendent—or maybe even see both the tangible and the transcendent in the same light?

PART IV:
OUR RUNTIME NARRATIVES

16

Software and stories

Now that we've ascended to the lofty heights of building a software-based model for the entire universe and the intelligent beings that inhabit it, let's come back down to Earth and take a look at good ol' computer software again. More specifically, let's more closely re-examine what happens when a particular piece of software runs on a particular device.

Consider, for example, your navigation app. When you run that app on your phone, you don't see streams of 0s and 1s on your screen. That is, you don't see the code. You see what the code does. Actually, you see what the code tells a bunch of logic gates to do, and those logic gates in turn tell your device's operating system what to do. The operating system then directs all the functional components of your device—its display, built-in GPS, mathematical calculating capabilities, access to data in memory, audio functions, security, etc.—to work in concert to provide you with a certain "user experience."

The operating system, in other words, is itself a very sophisticated piece of software comprised of many distinct modules that each have their own function but are also designed to coordinate very closely with each other.

You input your request to the navigation app for directions. This causes a stream of code to run through the logic gates. The logic gates drive the operating system. The operating system, among other things, causes your device to display a certain image on its screen. That display includes the names of streets and landmarks, the highlighting of a chosen route, and colors to represent land and water. The code may also tell the logic gates to tell the operating system to tell the audio function of your device to speak to you in an annoying synthesized voice with instructions about where and when to turn.

To mark the route you need to follow, your device must display that road in a color that differentiates it from the other roads on the device's screen. And to make sure you can see that the name of the road you need to follow on that route is Highway 61, your device must precisely display all the pixels of the characters in the label "Highway 61" in a color that differentiates it from the color of the route itself.

But the navigation app's code doesn't have to specify exactly what color to use for every single pixel on your device's display. That would be extraordinarily inefficient. Instead, the code for the app instructs your device's operating system to fetch the names of the roads on your map from a reference database. The pixels for each character in "Highway 61" are thus chunked as complete alphanumeric characters.

So your device doesn't have to figure out for itself that the capital "H" consists of pixels arranged in two long vertical lines connected by pixels arranged in a shorter horizontal line. Nor does it have to calculate from scratch exactly how to rotate those lines in order to display "Highway 61" at various angles as you drive along your route. The letter "H" is chunked into alphanumeric code—along with the rest of the letters in "Highway 61," which is chunked as a road name.

The colored highlighting of your selected route is similarly chunked. The software doesn't figure out how to draw the map and then figure out how to put a nice purple squiggle on it that perfectly matches the lines and curves of your selected route. It simply identifies the roads on your route and displays them in the color globally assigned to the set of pixels chunked as "selected route."

In other words, while at its lowest level, your app's code is a set of many 0s and 1s, your app as a whole has a certain natural chunked logic to it. That chunked logic is specifically chunked to streamline the task of showing you where you are and where you need to go.

Once upon an app

Software developers have a term they often use to describe the logical chunks they string together to fulfill a particular purpose. They call them "stories." The basic "story" for navigation software is "The user wants to see how to get from Point A to Point B." But there are many variations on this story. These variations can include "The user wants to see how to get from Point A to Point B in the least amount of time," "The user wants see how to get from Point A to Point B without paying any tolls," and "The user wants to see how to get from Point A to Point B to Point C."

These stories describe your intended subjective experience with the app. You ask the app to get you from where you are now to somewhere else—and you specify speed as opposed to toll avoidance. Then, as you drive, you listen to its instructions and occasionally check its display. The runtime of the app makes sense to you not as a sequence of properly ordered 0s and 1s, but as a "story."

Of course, when we hear the word "story," it's easy to first think about something that's totally fictional—like the story of The Three Bears or the plot of The Maltese Falcon. Stories can indeed be entirely fictional. They can also be entirely factual—such as when someone tells you a story about their workday or their vacation (assuming that they're honest, of course).

Stories can also be part fact and part fiction. Sometimes we forget certain details. Sometimes we embellish them to enhance their drama. Sometimes we aren't 100% sure of certain sections, so we insert what we believe was most likely to have occurred at that particular juncture. The word "story" includes all of these cases and more.

We also tend to think of stories as being sequential. That's why we start them off with framings like "Once upon a time…" or "Last week, when I was talking to my friend Brad Pitt…" But while this is largely true, for our purposes here, I'm going to not burden the term "story" with that constraint. If you ask me to describe my living space, I'm also going to tell you a "story"—even though I don't relate a series of events over time. Stories, after all, can include descriptions in addition to plots. They can also jump around in time to fill in backstories or to enhance dramatic effect.

In the case of software development, stories help teams understand what the app they're writing is supposed to accomplish—and all the various circumstances users may encounter as they use that app. A development team working on an app may consider a user story like this:

> *"A not-very-tech-literate customer comes to our site looking for Product A, but while browsing finds a Product B that they like. So they want to somehow save Product B for future reference while they continue shopping for Product A."*

Once developers write the code for this story, they can then test it to see if it works—that is, if it successfully does what the story describes. Note that the story isn't about calls to a database, caching an SKU, or colors on a display. It's an abstraction of the underlying code that describes how that code should be functionally experienced by a real, live person.

The key thing about stories is that they are narratives that express what code *does* when it runs. In doing so, software stories insulate us from the awful complexity of what the code *is* and *how* it runs.

17

Stories we tell ourselves

We can apply this same concept of insulating narratives to the interactions between ourselves and our universe. After all, our consciousness needs to efficiently process the code of the cosmos in much the same way as a device has to process the code of an app.

To better understand the way our own insulating narratives enable us to function in an otherwise impossibly complex cosmos, let's look at three types of stories in particular. The first two we'll examine briefly here. The third we'll save for the next chapter.

Personal stories

We're not all novelists or screenwriters, but we're telling ourselves stories all the time. And many of the stories we tell ourselves are about ourselves.

The entirety of all the code that makes us us—our DNA, its outward expression in our physical characteristics, our relationships with family members and others, our relationships to all the events we've experienced from the moment we were born—is way too extensive and complex for us to completely and granularly process at any given moment. So we distill that code into a story of manageable size and simplicity. We chunk ourselves in order to understand ourselves.

We all take a different approach to our personal "me-ness" stories. Some people strongly identify with their parents, family, and nationality/ethnic group. Others have me-ness narratives that strongly de-identify with those entities. Physical features, special talents, childhood trauma, and personal achievement play a larger role in some people's stories than in others.

Our me-ness narratives can change over time. Many of us have even discovered in therapy that some aspects of the story we kept telling ourselves about ourselves were killing us—so we had to intentionally and significantly change the me-ness stories in our heads.

But regardless of what your personal story may be, it is your story. It is not inclusive of every 0 and 1 of code that your life has processed and is processing. It is instead the means by which you translate that incredibly complex underlying code into the chunked narrative you call "me."

Historical narratives

History is an especially interesting case of story-making. Technically, it's probably safe to say that there is only one "true" version of history: that which includes every event that has ever occurred in precise chronological order, with completely accurate and hyper-granular assertions about causes and effects.

But, of course, that version of history is unknowable and untellable. It would also most likely lack meaning—since it wouldn't differentiate between the assassination of Archduke Franz Ferdinand and the umpteenth time it took you more than five minutes to find your car keys.

So we craft narratives from the assorted facts and falsehoods we learn over the years—along with the various interpretations we receive about those facts and falsehoods. If you're an American citizen, your version of history may include a narrative about the heroic origin of a nation founded by freedom-loving British colonists influenced by the political philosophies of the Enlightenment. On the other hand, you may think of your nation as conceived in the genocide of indigenous inhabitants and the enslavement of imported ones. Or your narrative may combine both sets of facts and associated interpretations in some proportion.

Regardless of our personal nationality, politics, or temperament, though, we all write historical narratives that are essentially our "reading" of whatever data we have as input.

This is not to say that every reading of history is of equal validity. I personally have serious doubts about readings of history that excessively romanticize the past. And it is certainly inaccurate to say that the Visigoth king Alaric I sacked Rome, New York in 1744.

But it is reasonable to assert that every reading of history is a synthesized story, rather than pure unadulterated capital-H History itself. We can't process all the code of historical time. That's why we have no choice as conscious beings but to experience the code of history as chunked and filtered narrative.

The third type of narrative that I believe warrants a closer look is scientific narrative. But that one deserves its own dedicated chapter.

18

Science as story

While you may be open to the idea that we understand people and history in terms of stories that are often imprecise to some degree or another, you might be a bit resistant to the notion that the field of inquiry we call "science" is also a set of chunked narratives that don't have to be 100% true to be useful—but instead only have to be "true enough for now."

A single chapter is, of course, absurdly insufficient to take on the entire philosophy of science. But for our purposes here, it will be useful to frame science in our present context of software and story.

A working definition

People use the word "science" in many ways. Some use it to refer the natural sciences: biology, chemistry, physics, etc. Others expand it to include fields such as social science and economics—with the caveat that such endeavors are only "scientific" insofar as they involve rigorous quantification, repeatability, and peer review.

Idiomatic usage of the word goes as far as to call boxing "the sweet science." More recently, some in the scientific community have sought to narrow the definition of science to exclude the work of theoretical physicists who speculate about the underlying nature of things using purely mathematical and logical arguments, rather than experimentation *per se*.

For our purposes here, I'd like to propose a working definition of science that has three components:

1) **Science is the activity of investigating empirically observable phenomena.** Defining science as an activity—instead of a body of knowledge—allows us to include in our definition all the things that scientists have historically been both right and wrong about. That is, it rightly frames science as a progressive quest for knowledge via the scientific method, even though that method is at times imperfectly applied by imperfect people.

2) **Science continuously self-corrects through falsification.** This second component of our definition highlights the fact that science is non-dogmatic about its assertions of fact—although its assertions about method are in a sense "dogmas." Self-correction through falsification also underscores the progressive nature of scientific inquiry, along with the fact that the domain of science is restricted to assertions that can at least potentially be falsified by empirical disproof.[19]

3) **Science is strictly narrative.** Science doesn't make ethical judgements or offer prescriptive advice. It describes the world with explanatory tools that align with available evidence. So it can describe the efficacy of a treatment for cancer without necessarily telling us how to balance the efficacy of those treatments against their side-effects or how much patients should be charged for them. Science doesn't even have to precisely explain exactly how a treatment works. It can simply tell the story "When we do X, Y happens Z percent of the time."

---

[19] The concept of falsifiability was introduced by the philosopher Karl Popper in 1934. It is a key element in our current understanding of scientific truth as being limited to assertions that can theoretically be proven untrue. The assertion "All swans are white," for example, can be disproven by the observation of a black swan.

Rigor in our definition of science is important to avoid unconsciously lapsing into a tautology along the lines of "science is everything that is objectively true, and everything that is objectively true is science." Mathematics isn't science. Neither is moral philosophy. The philosophy of science isn't even science. Science can't prove the validity of its own scientific method—which in fact depends on metaphysical arguments. So we must place proper bounds around our definition of science and not make excessive claims on its behalf.

Narratives of the tangible

Here's an example that may help clarify this notion of science as a human activity whereby narrative truths are progressively advanced over time.

Philosophers of ancient Greece and India speculated about the unit of matter we now call the "atom" centuries before the advent of what we now know as the scientific method. As the scientific revolution progressed, a more modern notion of atomism was conceived by Boscovich, Dalton, and others.

Eventually, through the work of physicists such as Thomson, Rutherford, and Bohr, a model of an atom comprised of a nucleus and orbiting electrons emerged. This image of the atom as a sort of miniature solar system with the nucleus as its sun and electrons as its planets remains familiar to most of us today—and still serves as a useful way to describe matter for many purposes.

In fact, equipped with the Bohr model, you can do all kinds of nifty things. You can better understand chemical bonds. You can create new elements. You can build very powerful bombs.

But, while the Bohr model provides a useful narrative description of what an atom is, it has proven to be incomplete and certainly less than accurate. Today, we no longer understand protons and neutrons to be the irreducible components of the nucleus. Our spatial understanding of electrons has evolved from a knowable orbit to quantum theory's probabilistic distribution. Our understanding of the relationships between forces that govern interactions between subatomic particles also continues to evolve.

In other words, the Bohr model was a good and useful story, even though it wasn't "true" in the deepest sense of the word. The same could be said of Newtonian physics—which is "true" only at a certain scale.

Interestingly, our ongoing investigation into the nature of the universe at both subatomic and galactic scales—our quest for a so-called "theory of everything"—seems to be driven by an innate desire for narrative coherence. We want a model that unites our currently disparate story lines, so we devote considerable intellectual energies and engineering resources to discovering exactly that. There is, however, no scientific reason that science should pursue such ends. That pursuit is driven by an *a priori* metaphysical, philosophical, or perhaps even esthetic position.

And, of course, science really gets it wrong sometimes. The history of science is littered with ideas such as ether, phlogiston, and phrenology. Many of us took the evolutionary maxim "survival of the fittest" to be as true as true could be, until philosophers of science pointed out that the maxim was in fact a meaningless tautology—because we were simply defining the "fittest" as those that survived. So "survival of the fittest" essentially means nothing more than that the fit are fit—and survivors survive.

None of this is to diminish the scientific enterprise in the least. On the contrary, science's ability to develop viable stories about tangible phenomena has yielded incalculable benefits to our species—and may ultimately be instrumental in ensuring that life on our planet survives.

But science is stories. And the stories of science are not the full set of all true and/or useful stories. In fact, as Gödel might have put it, science itself is a story that is not a story of science.

19

Is all knowledge narrative?

Why is this important? How does the framing of science and scientific inquiry as narrative support the stated purpose of this book—which is to bring the tangible and the transcendent together into a single, common realm of reason?

For one thing, this narrative framing suggests something we might term "epistemic unity." That is, while there are certainly major differences between studying organic chemistry and painting landscapes—and while the utility of one is certainly different from the utility of the other—as human activities they must also have something in common. Both, after all, entail the engagement of an individual human consciousness with a cosmos of inconceivable vastness and complexity. Heck, sometimes it's the very same individual human who both studies and paints.

It is thus my contention that both studying and painting—both science and art—share something deeply significant: *the use of narrative to coherently chunk incomprehensibly complex code.* When they look at the natural world, neither the scientist nor the artist reads the underlying code of the world. They process the code of the world through their respective consciousnesses to create their respective maps of the world as they perceive it. But in neither case is the map of the world that they create the world itself.

For another, narrative framing disabuses us of the notion that the only "real knowledge" is perfected scientific knowledge. Math is not science, yet it produces verifiably true assertions. Your visual perception of a traffic light's redness is not subject to independent empirical observation, but it occurs nonetheless. And your subjective qualia-resident narrative regarding the redness of that light better be accurate, or someone could get badly hurt in a car accident. The injustice of wrongful imprisonment is no less unjust because it evades clinical quantification. Science doesn't tell us that we shouldn't jail the innocent. Nonetheless, we know we shouldn't do it.

All knowledge, in other words—whether personal, social, scientific, moral, or esthetic—is *a pursuit of usefully chunked explanatory narratives that overlay the transcendent, impossibly complex software of a relational cosmos that we can never directly observe but that is always acting upon us.* The methods, purviews, and outcomes of our diverse knowledge disciplines may differ significantly, but knowledge itself is a single thing—as is the cosmos that our knowledge attempts to know.

It's worth noting that even entirely fictional narratives can serve as exceptional "containers" for truth. That's why novels, movies, TV series, song lyrics, and the like can be so compelling. It is through these fabricated stories that artists communicate significant truths about the cosmos. *Death of a Salesman* is not the true story of a real Willy Loman—but it's a story through which Arthur Miller nonetheless presents some compelling truths about people and the world.

Does it really make sense to arbitrarily segregate the "you" that absorbs the truths in *Death of a Salesman* from the "you" that knows the freezing point of water at sea level is 0° Celsius? Is the mind edified by the play not the same mind that checks the thermometer before deciding whether it's safe to skate on the lake?

When we understand the universe as software—and knowledge as narrative—we are no longer compelled to fragment our pursuit of knowledge into arbitrary categories. Nor are we any longer compelled to demote rational inquiry into the transcendent to some lower rank than rational inquiry into the empirical. We can escape both the former (dualism) and the latter (reductive materialism) without compromising our rationality or denigrating our direct experience of consciousness.

This twin liberation frees us to continue in our quest to understand our cosmos and ourselves. So freed, we may even find ourselves better equipped to rationally re-consider the transcendent—even as we continue to nurture and advance our ever-astonishing scientific knowledge.

PART V:
NARRATIVES OF THE DIVINE

20

Our story so far

We've covered a lot of territory in the first four parts of this book. And I appreciate you sticking with me over the course of what amounts to about 20,000 words so far. If you want to quit here, I'd like to think I've already given you plenty to think about.

But I'm hoping you'll stick with me for at least one more leg of this journey, because I'd like us to tackle what I believe is one of the thorniest issues that we face as human beings in the 21st century: rational engagement with the inherently transcendent aspects of the human experience.

Before we press on to the summit, however, let's briefly reconsider three key ideas that have emerged from our investigation into software as a model for understanding the cosmos.

Idea #1: The tangible world is comprised of relational code.

The chair you're sitting on right now seems solid and "something-y" enough, but it's really just a lot of subatomic nothings (or almost-nothings) acting upon each other in ways that give that chair its seemingly tangible properties. Chairs come in all shapes and sizes. We ultimately call what you're sitting on a "chair" (or a "couch" or a "bench" or whatever) because of its proportions in relation to your legs, back, and butt—and how you choose to relate to it functionally.

Your chair only appears to be the color it is because of how your personal optical system reads the wavelengths of light currently reflecting from its surface. Its materials only have the density and texture they do because of the way its molecules interact—how closely they fit together, how flexibly they can move against each other, etc. And the chair only weighs what it weighs because of the planet it happens to be on at the moment. The chair doesn't actually have any inherent weight at all. Its weight is simply a function of the relationship between its mass and the mass of Earth.

And while it's convenient enough for us to call it a chair, it is really its own very specific entity. It may be exactly like many other chairs manufactured at the same time and place—but it is not any of those chairs. Maybe it's a chair you own, a special chair where for years you've done your most serious reading and thinking. Maybe it's a chair in a coffee shop that has become your favorite chair. Or—tragedy of tragedies—maybe your favorite chair in the coffee shop is currently occupied by some ignoramus who doesn't realize that they've thoughtlessly displaced you into an entirely second-rate chair that is nowhere near as suitably positioned for chill coffee-shop reading and contemplation.

We can engage in this same exercise with tables, stones, buildings, cars, and computers. In everyday life, it's functionally convenient to perceive and use these things in the chunked manner that we humans do. But a little basic science and reason makes it clear that what is functionally convenient for humankind is not always what is phenomenologically true from the most rigorous and thoughtful perspective.

Idea #2: Consciousness is code running code.

Because we are as much inhabitants of the cosmos as any chair or table, we are similarly subject to its principles. So while it has become our daily habit to think of and operate ourselves as entities of independent substance, we too are comprised of nothings (or almost-nothings) in temporary, ever-fluid relations with each other.

Our brains may appear to be some kind of super-sophisticated computer hardware, but our conscious minds—that which is doing your reading and thinking right now—are not our brains. A better metaphor for consciousness is a highly complex operating system running highly complex software on the virtual machine of the brain.

Brains, after all, have the same relational makeup as any other matter—so they themselves are a kind of code. That's why people with certain brain injuries can sometimes regain mental capabilities by shifting functions to an uninjured portion of their brain's virtual hardware.

Personally, I tend to view consciousness as a virtual machine running on top of that virtual machine brain. That is, when brain scientists detect the impulses that travel through a person's brain as that person sees the color red, they are actually observing the virtual machine of the brain running the sensation module of the mind's operating system. The actual qualia of red that appears in a person's consciousness—their subjective experience of perception, if you will—is not evident in that scientific observation. The subjective self-awareness of our own perceptions is yet another layer of code-like transcendence.

Consciousness might then be understood as a virtual machine that runs on the virtual machine of the mind's operating system, which in turn runs on the virtual machine of the brain's physical reality.

Or not. The main point is that the physical hardware of your brain is not what's currently reading this book and exercising skepticism about its assertions. It is the software of your consciousness.

Idea #3: All knowledge is chunked narrative.

Given our software metaphor for the world and all that's in it, what does consciousness do? Simply put, consciousness encodes abstractions and instantiates runtimes.

We encode when we communicate outward. I'm encoding my thoughts right now to put them into a unitized format that I'm hoping you can run in a relatively ordered manner. We encode when we decide to make traffic lights turn red for "stop" and green for "go"—and to make stop signs both red and octagonal. We encode when we smile and shake hands in greeting a friend. Now, we may have entirely forgotten exactly why it is that handshakes have become a signifier of friendly greeting—but that doesn't matter. We've already chunked the code.

We execute runtimes when we interpret incoming signals. Our biological optical apparatus (eye, nerves, brain cells) sends a signal to the virtual machine of our brain that the incoming light is of a particular frequency. Our consciousness then chunks that code with the qualia of its color—unless, of course, we're colorblind.

Similarly, our auditory apparatus (eardrum, earbones, cochlea, nerves, brain cells) may send a signal to the virtual machine of our brains that a very hoarse voice is moaning musically about the terrible beauty of life. Our consciousness endows us with both the qualia associated with perception of that voice and the ability to recognize these qualia as characteristic of the singer Tom Waits—whose voice we then might associate with sweet drunken nights in a dorm room back in '77.

The key point here is that the runtimes of our consciousness are not direct dot-for-dot accurate-to-the-nth-degree-of-granularity depictions of some external reality. They are chunked stories. If you make sounds with your mouth that match the name "George

Washington," I don't process those sounds as the full and complete human being George Washington across the entirety of his earthly lifetime from 1732 AD to 1799 AD (dating which, it should be noted, is itself based on chronologically questionable religious narrative). I process your mouth-sounds as some idiosyncratically chunked subjective story I have created about the particular human being we all know as George Washington.

That story, that narrative, will differ from person to person. Some people's consciousnesses will chunk the name by invoking a great revolutionary leader. Some will invoke chunks about chopping down a cherry tree or crossing the Delaware. Some will chunk Washington as a symbol of slavery and patriarchy. Some consciousnesses will call up a chunk of narrative about false teeth from its database of narratives. The point is that Person A's operating system will run Person B's mouth-sound input in its own idiosyncratic way—regardless of what Person B may have been intending to communicate when they spoke Washington's name.

These subjective runtime narratives are not merely matters of differing opinion. Our personal experiences of consciousness also vary in the granularity and accuracy of what we can reasonably call objective truth. When you say "salt," my consciousness chunks the chemical formula NaCl. Not everyone does that, because not everyone was reading chemistry books in third grade.

Professional chemists will understand NaCl on much deeper terms than I do—so the chunked narrative they run in their consciousness will have scientific depth mine does not. Professional chefs, on the other hand, may call sub-program narratives that put salt in the relational context of cooking. Someone employed in public works may associate salt with icy roads. And, of course, if you make the mouth-sounds of "salt" to someone who doesn't understand English, you may just get a quizzical look—until you decide to re-encode the same abstraction by gesturing as though you are shaking salt onto a piece of food.

It's important to note that the use of chunked narrative is not a learned behavior. It is intrinsic to consciousness. Babies chunk their perceived reality into stories. Even animals chunk narratives in their own ways—though their chunking is likely much simpler and not tied to language in the same way that ours is. Without chunking, they wouldn't be able correlate inputs such as aromas and mating displays to their requisite agency in actions such as hunting or sex. Consciousness requires narrative for coherence, context, and agency. And the relational coherence of chunked narrative is what differentiates the functional software of mind from the chaos of the data deluge that the cosmos is endlessly spewing.

■ ■ ■

With this understanding of the cosmos as *code*, of consciousness as *code running code*, and of knowledge as *chunked narrative*—in tandem with our earlier investigation of *relational primacy*—we are ready to take our next step.

21

Fact and myth

Our next step requires that we make sure we at least temporarily put aside two common misconceptions—both of which we've already addressed. The first misconception is that scientific narratives regarding the *tangible* are of necessity "fully true" simply because the scientific community has reported that they have been tested by scientific method, undergone peer review, etc. As we have seen, this simply means that they are functionally viable chunked narratives of the code that underlies the cosmos. Scientific assertions may have to be revised based on future discoveries. They may be incomplete. In fact, the validity of the entire scientific enterprise is based on the willingness to view all assertions of scientific fact as subject to future falsification. That's why science is science—rather than dogma.

The second common misconception is that narratives regarding the *transcendent* are of necessity "fully incapable of being assigned any truth-rating whatsoever" because their origin is something other than the empirically based scientific method. If someone says, "I love you," they are making an assertion that cannot be empirically proven. But you'll probably be able to assign some kind of truth-rating to their assertion sooner or later.

In fact, we constantly assess the truth-rating of assertions using a wide range of criteria other than either the scientific method or a pure leap of faith. We can rightly determine that a knowledge-story about the Colorado National Guard firing on striking coal miners in

Ludlow, Colorado on April 20, 1914 is much truer than a knowledge-story about how extraterrestrial lizard overlords control the U.S. Federal Reserve Bank. But we should assess the truthfulness of these knowledge-stories based on rational evaluation of their merits, rather than on snap judgements and/or prejudices regarding their origin.

We should also keep in mind that truthfulness is not purely binary. Some stories are entirely false. Some are entirely true. But many knowledge-stories contain elements of both truth and falsehood. We can therefore assign knowledge-stories truth-ratings that range across whatever scale we create—say, from a 0 of total falsehood to a perfect 10 of absolute accuracy—regardless whether those knowledge-stories originate from biology, mathematics, literature, or the person who's talking our ear off while we're stuck next to them on a four-hour flight.

How true are "fact" stories?

We've already spent some time looking at scientific truth as functional narrative—but let's take a few moments to make our understanding of "fact" as clear as possible. Scientific facts are knowledge-stories that arise from the collective activity of a group of people we call "scientists." These people are supposed to use specific empirical methods to gain knowledge of the phenomenological world. They also rationally speculate about the world in order to construct theories that can (they hope) eventually be verified or falsified through experiment and observation.

The body of scientific knowledge-stories at any given time includes four types of narratives: 1) those that are accepted as true today and will continue to be so accepted, 2) those that are accepted as true today, but will be falsified sometime in the future, 3) narratives about which disagreement exists and will continue to exist for some period of time, and 4) bogus science.

Some of us might consider phlogiston to be a type 4 knowledge-story, although it was certainly held to be true by some percentage of the scientific community for a while. There's also a possibility that the assertion "No communication can occur across space faster than the speed of light"—which just about everybody thought would forever be a type 1 knowledge-story—is now headed to type 2 status given recent observations regarding quantum entanglement.[20]

As previously noted, we had a knowledge-story about the atom that was functional enough for some of what we wanted to do—but we then revised it. We treated Newton's mathematical models as gospel until we didn't. We had a working knowledge-story for the mass of the cosmos, but we revised that story to accommodate first "dark matter" and then "dark energy." We will likely have to revise these stories again.

This endless editing and re-editing of scientific knowledge-stories is not limited to advanced physics. My periodontist once shared with me some clinical research indicating that dental plaque could lead to heart disease. Shortly thereafter, I met a well-respected cardiologist at a party who responded to the topic with eye-rolls. What was I to make of that knowledge-story given the differing viewpoints of two highly qualified medical professionals?

History, as we have seen, can be especially gray on our truth-rating scale. I was taught as a child that Columbus "discovered" America. Later I learned that he never even reached the North American mainland, that Leif Erikson and others probably got there before he

---

[20] Quantum entanglement—which Einstein referred to as "spooky action at a distance"—occurs when the quantum state of two or more particles are inextricably linked, despite their spatial separation. While that linkage may be due to correlation rather than causation, the linkage still suggests that state information could conceivably be used to overcome the theoretical limit of lightspeed transmission.

did, and that you can't discover a land that is already inhabited by human beings with rich civilization and culture.

Economics and the social sciences offer similar examples. Capitalists herald themselves as "job creators"—but then we crunch the numbers and see how often investors create wealth by eliminating labor. Educators of a certain ilk swear by "whole language" as the best way to teach kids to read, despite anecdotal evidence that they can be outperformed by practitioners of classic phonics.

And so it goes. It's certainly true that your car needs lubrication. But beware of a knowledge-story that would have you change your oil more than you need to—especially if that knowledge-story comes from the person selling you the motor oil. Does a surgeon recommend surgery? Get a second opinion.

None of this is to say that those who assert knowledge-stories with less than a perfect truth-rating are scammers, liars, or fools. But we should be clear about the fact that narrative truth-values are not limited to just "totally true" and "totally false." Many knowledge-stories are functionally useful even though they are incomplete, biased, or just plain wrong in ways that don't interfere with their utility. And many knowledge-stories are pretty useless even though they may be wholly true.

How false are myths?

Now let's consider narratives some of us might be especially prone to dismiss out of hand—and that others might ask us to accept wholly "by faith."

As one example, consider the opening words of St. John's gospel in the Christian scriptures. As typically translated into English, the opening line of this narrative is "In the beginning was the Word."

The word "Word" in this translation is a weak attempt to convey the meaning of "logos" in the early Koine Greek texts. "Logos" is not semantically equivalent to the English word "word." It carries a stronger sense of underlying principle, reasoning, or computation. Like "word," "logos" implies something that can be spoken—but the spoken "logos" is much more than a mundane word. It is a "word" in the highest sense of something deep and powerful manifesting itself in the clothing of syllable.

If one were so inclined, one might even be tempted to translate "logos" as "code." After all, as we have seen, words are a kind of code—and code captures the sense of "logos" as a kind of ur-communication that possesses the power of agency.

More to the point, if we ascribe to the notion of the Big Bang as the moment when the essential nature of the present universe—its physics, and therefore by extension all of its chemistry and biology— was fully encoded in some kind of unfathomable initial explosive expansion, then it makes even more sense to understand "logos" as a kind of cosmos-initiating code event.

Armed with this reading of Christianity's most sacred text, we might give St. John's opening line a reasonable bit of respect—if not outright awe—rather dismissing it as the scribbling of a wacked-out Judean mystic. How was it that more than a millennium before Arno Penzias and Robert Wilson first picked up the faint microwave echoes of the Big Bang, some guy living in a backwater of the Roman Empire was able to so elegantly describe a knowledge-story of cosmogony with such a surprisingly high truth-value?

And perhaps in this context, it wouldn't hurt to consider the possible truth-value that we might assign to the next line of John's account: "And the Code was with God and the Code *was* God."

22

Myth and mountain

Of course, I can be accused of cherry-picking the narrative example at the end of the last chapter to support my thesis about software and transcendence. And I'm guilty as charged. Few religious texts correlate so wonderfully with the concept of a software-like cosmogony as the opening line of John's Gospel.

But the point of this exercise isn't to make a universal claim of high truth-value for all religious texts—or for the Christian canon. All we've done is demonstrate that narrative assertions can't automatically be assigned truth-ratings based on their topic or origin. John being right about something doesn't make him right about everything. And Einstein being wrong about something doesn't make him wrong about everything. Truth-ratings should be based on evidence and reason—not irrelevant attributes of their source.[21]

Just as important, narratives that use poetic or metaphorical language to make assertions about the transcendent cannot be assigned truth-ratings of zero simply because they were not written in a more straightforward prose style. In fact, as we have seen, all language is ultimately metaphorical in nature—since it does not precisely correspond to what it purports to describe. "Red" is a useful signifier for the qualia we experience when we see certain wavelengths of

---

[21] Arguing that an assertion is false simply because the person who said it has been known to lie or be less than accurate in previous statements is the classic logical fallacy of *argumentum ad hominem*.

light, but it doesn't accurately describe what the phenomenon of red light is. "Home" is a chunked container for places with which people have certain types of transcendent, empirically unobservable relationships—but it also represents something ineffably metaphorical about "where the heart is." "Hot" is more than just objectively measurable temperature; it can also refer to a social trend, sexually attractive appearance, or stolen goods.

Given the fundamentally metaphorical nature of language, let's consider more examples of mythic narrative. Many cultures assign divine attributes to major local topographic features, especially mountains—two examples being Mount Everest (or *Chomolungma* to the Sherpa people) and the four sacred mountains of the Navajo.

Let's also agree for the sake of this exercise that the truth-ratings of these narratives are less than a full ten out of ten—i.e., that these mountains are not "gods" in the precise sense that we might understand the word "gods."

Does that mean we should automatically assign these knowledge-stories a truth-rating of absolute zero? Might we be able to mine some truth from these stories? Could these mythic narratives potentially have some value to us as we grapple with the transcendent? Or, to couch it in the language we've been using in this book, can such narratives help us chunk some "good enough" stories out of the underlying code of the cosmos that escapes our limited powers of direct observation because it's both profoundly relational and profoundly complex?

I'd suggest that the answers to these questions is certainly "yes"—and that we should be very cautious about dismissing the mythic narratives of the Sherpa and Navajo out-of-hand. I am inclined to listen to what people who have lived in proximity to a great mountain for generation after generation tell me about that mountain—and about living in proximity to it. I am also inclined to assert that anyone who is truly curious about being human in the world should give heed to these narratives too.

Sure, the way other people encode their lived knowledge may not jibe perfectly with the operating system I personally have running in my own head. But if I put a little effort into code conversion[22]—or try running a emulation of someone else's operating system—I might learn something true about the relationship between a great mountain and those living consciously in the presence of that mountain.[23] I might even learn something about the mountain and me.

At the very least, mythic narratives tell us what the people who live by the mountain believe they know about the mountain. That is an anthropological fact in and of itself. And it is a non-trivial fact, because it encodes something about reality—i.e., that people living in the presence of the mountain are relationally affected by that presence in some specific ways.

Actually, having traveled among and lived with mountain people, I have first-hand anecdotal evidence that there is something about them that is different from people who live on open inland plains or on ocean shores—and that their stories offer insight into these differences. I also have ample independent evidence from anthropologists, novelists, musicologists, and others to support my case.[24]

---

[22] In computer software, we sometimes call this kind of code conversion "re-platforming." It is something older corporations often struggle with as their core business applications get a bit long in the tooth. Re-platforming large, complex applications from older platforms—such as programs written in the COBOL language to run on IBM mainframe—often proves to be challenging and expensive. The metaphor of re-platforming for those of us who have thought one way and/or lived in one culture for an extended period of time is pretty obvious.

[23] Or the relationship between the jar and Tennessee, as per the Stevens poem.

[24] There is certainly evidence that the phonemes of different languages are often the result of geographical features. See, for example, Caleb Everett's work on the Evidence for Direct Geographic Influences on Linguistic Sounds.

We may, of course, have trouble putting our finger on the exact nature of mountain-relationality. And we may argue about its specifics. But it's not really reasonable to deny that the constant, looming presence of a mighty mountain jutting majestically into the sky has zero discernible effect on the people who have been living in its shadow for centuries. And that effect, that force, is transcendent. It is not directly observable by empirical means.

We may be able to see how the mountain affects a people's diet, housing, and culture. But we cannot see their subjective mountain-based qualia. We need to hear their stories to access that code.

It's also worth noting that a mountain like Everest doesn't just impact the Sherpa. It also affects non-Sherpas who climb it or merely attempt to climb it. Even those who spend mere hours contemplating Everest's immensity from a distance can feel its effect on them in the moment—and perhaps even for the rest of their lives. So it's not just mountain people who experience the transcendence of mountain-relationality. It's anyone who is open to the reality of the transcendent.

Of course, there may be some people who see Everest and are unaffected by it in any conscious or unconscious way. But that appears to be a deficit of consciousness, rather than a superior or more truthful way of being in the world.

The dismissive assertion that mythic mountain-narratives should be given a truth-rating of zero simply because they are mythic narratives of local cultures is one that itself may warrant a truth-rating of zero. Such dismissal may well be based on something other than reason. That's why we should all examine our preconceptions about myth— and re-consider any tendency we have to dismiss the metaphorical knowledge-stories of others.

23

Myth and math

There is another branch of human knowledge that we should take a much closer look at before we go any further in our exploration of the transcendent: mathematics.

Math is relevant to our discussion for several reasons. For one thing, math is expressed symbolically—so it's perhaps the epitome of encoded knowledge. For another, math straddles the tangible and the transcendent. It's certainly a very useful tool for the scientific investigation of the tangible. We use math constantly quantify our observations of the world so we can accurately test our hypotheses. We also use math every day to cut sheetrock and figure out if the "super economy size" package at the supermarket is really the best deal.

But math itself is not science. That is, it is not based on empirical observation. We don't repeatedly experiment with various objects to discover what happens if we put 5001 of them in a box and then throw in another 5001. We understand through the abstract principles of mathematics that the result will be 10,002 objects.

When you're a child, an adult may use objects to illustrate to you that one apple plus one apple equals two apples. But you are quickly led to treat numerals as abstractions, so that "1+1=2" becomes a truth assertion on its own, independent of any underlying empirical phenomenon.

On the other hand, the mathematical assertion "1+1=2" is unlike the other transcendent assertions we've considered, because it is plainly objective. As long as I don't have any severe cognitive difficulties in regards to number-concepts, we can't really say that my understanding of math is contingent on some subjective, qualia-resident experience.

This is not to say that no subjective qualia arise in my consciousness when I read the symbols "1," "2," "+," and "=" on a piece of paper or computer screen. They do. But there isn't anything subjective about my understanding of the mathematical concepts they represent. One is one, plus is plus, equals is equals, and two is two.

The subjective qualia-based associations that arise in my consciousness when I read "1+1=2"—a blackboard in a classroom of my childhood, a dumb pop song, etc.—don't interfere with my ability to understand the symbol "1" as a direct correlate of the numerical value "1." This is why consciousness of "1" is quite different from consciousness of "red," "George Washington," or "mountain" as we've examined previously. We know that the primary attribute of the "1" that I encode will correlate pretty precisely with the "1" that you decode.

The precision of this symbolic correlation leads to still another reason that math is an important special case of knowledge-stories. Math comes as close as anything to delivering narratives with a truth-rating of a perfect 10. One plus one really does equal two.[25]

The coded narratives of mathematics yield such a high truth-rating precisely because they are narratives about pure abstraction. As we saw in our opening chapters about software, when I encode anything that isn't abstract (such as a product I'm selling online), I first have to create an abstraction of it using the values of my code-system (such as 0s and 1s in the case of computer code).

---

[25] Again, math nerds, I know that in binary notation 1+1=10—but we're trying to deal with core concepts here, not accidents of notation. For that matter, I plus I equals II. So there! ☺

But with math, the stories we tell are themselves already about pure abstractions—and they are told in a language or code specifically designed for those specific abstractions. This unique correlation between *what* mathematics communicates and *how* mathematics communicates makes math a very exceptional case of software and story.

The curious case of *i*

Math is so useful for making accurate assertions about pure abstraction that we can even invent symbols for concepts that seemingly have no correlate at all in the real world. The symbol *i* is a great example. It represents "the square root of -1." We came up with that concept and that symbol because in our earlier understanding of multiplication, no number multiplied by itself could yield a negative number. So we created the concept of a number that multiplied by itself could yield a negative number and gave it a coding value: *i*.

Then guess what happened? We actually found practical uses for *i* in all kinds of scientific endeavors, from electrical engineering to meteorology.

The curious case of *i* highlights the fact that we often conceive of true assertions long before we can fully understand or empirically prove them. John made an assertion in his gospel about the Big Bang long before anyone had any real evidence for it. Einstein started developing his ideas about relativity by simply imagining what it would be like to travel away from a clock at the speed of light. Experimental evidence supporting his assertions came much later.

Put another way, we can develop narrative assertions that have a very high truth-rating *a priori*[26] — without first having direct empirical encounters with them.

---

[26] For more on *a priori* vs. *a posteriori* knowledge, read Kant—or read something that explains some Kant for you.

This is not to say that every mathematical assertion warrants a perfect truth-rating of ten out of ten. You may have been taught in a middle-school geometry class, for example, that parallel lines never meet. And that will get you through as much geometry as most of us need to know in our earthly frame of reference.

But if you keep delving deeper, you'll eventually learn about non-Euclidean geometries in which parallel lines meet at one point in the infinite distance—or even two points at two infinite distances. So do we give Euclidean postulates a truth-rating of ten? Maybe, maybe not. But one plus one is always two. Unless, of course, you smush one and one together so hard that they just make another one that's twice as big.

24

Coding the divine

So now let's talk about the divine. We lightly touched on the topic of the divine when we looked at John's cosmogony and the deification of natural phenomena such as mountains by local peoples. But now it's time to take another big step.

And don't worry. I'm not going to try proselytizing you. I'm merely going to suggest that there may be something fundamentally transcendent about the cosmos that wouldn't be irrational to reify as "divine" or "divinity."

By the way, there's a reason I prefer to use words like "divine" and "divinity," rather than "God." Many of you closely associate the G-word with a highly anthropomorphized concept of a particular religion's deity. The word "divinity" may therefore be more useful for our present purpose, which is to better understand the transcendent by applying lessons we learn from software. Don't worry. I'm not going to evangelize any particular religion's dogmas.

I am also well-aware that you, valued reader, may have some specific God-concepts that you are adamantly for and/or adamantly against. By discussing divinity in more general terms, I hope we can steer clear of such sectarian disputes—and actually accomplish something important that will be valuable for us all.

But now that we've progressed this far as in our discussion of software and transcendence, we might as well tackle the notion of divinity—as well as religious teachings about divinity[27]—since that notion may be the quintessential case of humankind's grappling with the "something more" of the cosmos.

Divinity as narrative

First off, it will be helpful for us to make sure we place human conceptions of divinity into the appropriate context. This context is one that divinity narratives share with all other endeavors of human consciousness: They are knowledge-stories.

No concept of the divine can purport to directly, fully, and accurately capture whatever objective external reality of divinity may exist—any more than even the best biography of George Washington can purport to directly, fully, and accurately capture the objective, external reality of George Washington. Chunked narrative is awesome for communications between consciousnesses, but none of us should make excessive claims about the truth-value of our knowledge-stories—whether they're about God or George Washington.

Whatever we think and say about the divine is simply a way for us to discuss transcendence using the same kind of shorthand we use when we say that a car is red. Of course, the car isn't red. It is composed of parts that reflect light in many different ways. The pistons aren't red. Neither is the exhaust system. But most of the external surface of the car has been covered with a pigment that in ambient sunlight reflects wavelengths of 635-740 nm. So, yes, in that sense the car is "red." But let's not forget or minimize the fact that the redness of the car is a chunked narrative of convenience.

---

[27] Another possibly useful term here is "Godhead," which also refers to "godhood" or divinity.

We will consider our ability to assess the truth-rating of divinity narratives later. The first order of business, though, is to locate those narratives where they belong: in the company of all our other narratives. We may arrive at our divinity narratives using methods that differ somewhat from those we use to we arrive at our science narratives, our history narratives, our math narratives, and our narratives of self. But the end-product of all those methods is still narrative. All knowledge is story.

The code of all codes

Returning to the original premise of this book—that software provides an apt metaphor for us to think about the transcendent—it's no coincidence that the attributes theologians have historically associated with the divine are also attributes that we can associate with code. For example:

- *Transcendence.* We've been using this word as a metaphysical term throughout the book. But it's also a theological term. "Transcendence" in a theological context means that the divine is not tangible. It has no tangible existence. And, as we have seen, the same can be said of software. Code is not a tangible form of empirically observable matter or energy. It defies such observation.

  Most theologians would make the same assertion about the divine. Some religions even forbid any visual depiction of their deity for this very reason. Such a depiction would deny the transcendence of the divine by stooping to material representation.

- **Immanence.** "Immanence" as a theological term refers to the presence of a Supreme Being.[28] This presence is often contrasted with transcendence. There even is a bit of a conundrum as to how a deity could be both fully apart from the material world and fully present within it.

  Here again, software offers a more-than-useful exemplar. Software is very much "present" in the world. You may be using it right now. Ethereal 0s and 1s may even be passing through your body as you read through the instantiation of code via a WiFi, Bluetooth, or cellular signal. That signal itself is not transcendent, because it could be detected with the right kind of monitor. But the code carried by that signal is simultaneously both transcendent and immanent.

  More to the point, the qualia you're experiencing right now is most assuredly transcendent—since it can't be independently observed. Yet at the same time it's also as immanent as anything could possibly be, because it's right there in your consciousness. The software of qualia thus offers a great example of how something can be both empirically undetectable (transcendent) and inarguably "with you" (immanent).[29]

- **Omnipresence.** "Omnipresence" refers to the notion of that divinity is immanent everywhere simultaneously. This is clearly the case with the software of the cosmos—i.e., the coded attributes of quarks, the gravitational relations of

---

[28] The etymologically related name "Immanuel" (or "Emanuel") can be translated as "God with us."

[29] I'll suggest that there is also an analogy between a) the ur-code of divinity possessing the seemingly contradictory properties of transcendence and immanence and b) quantum theory's assertions regarding the seemingly contradictory properties of particle-ness and wave-ness.

celestial bodies, etc. That code is everywhere, acting on every point in the universe all the time.

We can, however, also think of all the computer code in the world as a single nebulous entity extending its presence across all instances of software everywhere. After all, when you make an in-game purchase on your smartphone, the software in your device is connected pretty seamlessly to the software running on the game's main servers, which is in turn connected to the software of a payment system that connects to transaction processing software running on a mainframe which connects to the software of the gaming company's bank-of-choice—and so on. We certainly seem to be on our way to making computer code omnipresent as we proliferate computing devices and data signals over the entire Earth and out into space.

Ultimately, though, it is the code of the cosmos that best correlates with the theological attribute of divine ubiquity.

- *Agency.* God, the theologians tell us, acts. Even Deists, who believe that God no longer needs to act presently in the world because the original act of setting the cosmic clockwork into motion was sufficient (a sort of "Big Bang" god), still attribute that original agency to the divine. And as we have seen, software similarly possesses agency—despite its immateriality. Agency is an attribute of code whether we consider software in its conventional sense or in the more universal way offered in this book.

Theologies, of course, differ greatly from religion to religion, from belief-system to belief-system. But the above examples suggest that at least some core knowledge-stories about the divine closely align with our knowledge-stories about software. ***Code works well as a narrative analog to divinity.*** And narrative analogs are ultimately all our human consciousness can offer in the way of knowledge.

25

Doing theology

In the previous chapter, we saw how knowledge-stories about software relate to knowledge-stories about divinity. But can we go further? Can we rationally explore the truth-value of knowledge-stories about the divine? That is, is a shared public theology even possible? And what purpose would such theology serve?

I suggest that rational discourse about theological narratives certainly is possible—with the caveat that we should be careful about the truth-ratings we assign to any such narrative. And one way I'll attempt to make a case for the validity of such discourse (assuming we're capable of asserting that "Narrative X seems to have some validity" rather than "Narrative X has a truth-rating of 10 and you will perish by my sword if you disagree") is by using the example of love.

Let's start by agreeing that love is a transcendent relational phenomenon. That is, we can't directly observe love itself (transcendence) and it occurs between entities (relational)[30].

I've personally experienced many kinds of love: familial, fraternal, romantic, puppy, etc. In some cases, I've navigated its mysteries with a bit of success. I've also experienced my share of failures. Perhaps your experience has been similar.

---

[30] We can consider self-love a special case of someone engaging relationally with themselves.

If you and I were to discuss love over dinner, however, I'm not sure if either of us could make an assertion about love that we would both agree has a truth-rating of 10. We might, however, agree in the negative. That is, we could affirm that certain assertions about love have a truth-rating of zero.

We might, for example, agree that bashing some random person on the head with a baseball bat could not rightly be defined as an act of love. We might also agree that it's not very loving to figuratively bash someone over the head with their past misdeeds or character flaws. We might not give the latter assertion a truth-rating of 10, however, because to "forgive and forget" is not always a cut-and-dried issue.

I might further suggest to you at this dinner that love entails sacrifice of one's own interests for the sake of one's beloved. You might counter with the point that to care for others one must also care for oneself. We might then debate a bit about self-sacrifice vs. self-care given our human limitations.

And so on. In this way, we could have a very worthwhile and mutually edifying conversation about love—even though neither one of us might be able to fully define what love is or make assertions that we could both agree merit a truth-rating of 10.

I would argue that dialog about the divine is quite similar. If I were to find my friend bowing before a bottle of shampoo, praying that it would bring about world peace, I might have some valid misgivings about their theology. If, on the other hand, someone were to tell me that God is love, I'd probably accept their assertion with some grace—even though I might not know exactly what they meant by either the word "God" or the word "love."

By the same token, I could probably have a very interesting and edifying conversation about the divine with someone who has studied the work of important modern theologians like Kapur Singh and

Vladimir Lossky—or someone who has been living out a spiritual belief through committed service to the poor.

The point here is not to argue for or against any particular theological principle. The point is that theology is, in fact, possible. Some theology is quite awful. Some theology can be quite rational. But the fact that there is so much bad theology doesn't mean that theology (or what we might term "inquiry into the divine") cannot ever be a reasonable endeavor—any more than the awful ways we hurt each other means that we should wholly reject the possibility of love.

A stab at the divine

By way of example, I'm going to offer three attributes of the divine to which I will admit partiality—along with my reasons for being partial to each.

Divinity as origin. I'm partial to the notion of divinity as precursor to and originator of the cosmos for several reasons. First and foremost, it supports the attribute of non-contingency. The divine isn't the divine if it's produced by a cause preceding itself. To be divine, in my way of modeling the cosmos, the divine must be some kind of pre-causal phenomenon. It can't depend on something being there first and then that something somehow making the divine greater and more transcendent than itself.[31]

Second, in my model of the cosmos as software, everything that exists must to some degree be coded into the Original Install Program™. And, as we have seen, there is plenty of scientific evidence that human intelligence itself (including our ability to observe and reason

---

[31] Put another way, it's fairly problematic to assert that the transcendent is an epiphenomenon of the tangible—rather than the other way around. Plus, for those understand the reference, I'll admit that I am not a huge fan of "turtles all the way down."

about the cosmos) was encoded as an evolutionary potentiality into the first moment of universal expansion.

Divinity as outside of time. The omnipresence of the divinity code in three-dimensional space seems to me to suggest omnipresence in four-dimensional space as well. Indeed, the divine may be omnipresent in dimensions beyond these, but at present I'm personally only familiar with the three dimensions of space and a fourth of time—so I won't speculate beyond those.

This seems to me to be a logical necessity for several reasons, including the fact that omnipresence in space *is* omnipresence in time—and that limiting divinity to speed-of-light travel is problematic when it comes to simultaneity in Boston and Bangkok.

Divinity as a multi-unity. I will also admit here to being trinitarian. There are several reasons why I like the number three more than the numbers two, four, or 5183—but the key notion here is a godhead that is both one and more than one. Conceptually, I assign multi-unity to the divine because I find the code metaphor so compelling—and for there to be any kind of "coding" to divinity, it must entail more than one "value."

Even more fundamentally, I find multi-unity necessary for any godhead to be inherently (or, more technically, non-contingently) relational. This non-contingent relationality is necessary because I view love as the fundamental relational value—and therefore inherent in the divine.

Now follow me here. A purely unitary concept of the divine would make divine love contingent on the existence of entities other than the divine. With a triune (or however-many-une you like) model, the godhead can love "internally"—i.e., without requiring that it first create an "external" object of that love—while avoiding any weirdly divine version of narcissism.

■ ■ ■

I'll also share the fact that I don't have a big problem with narrative runtimes that anthropomorphize the code of the divine. That is, I'm pretty OK with narratives that use human attributes to describe divine being and agency. This is in part because such anthropomorphized metaphors are probably pretty useful for communicating with anthros. When the Hebrew scriptures describe Yahweh as delivering the Israelites from Egypt "with a strong hand and an outstretched arm," I doubt we should take that description literally. But it may be a useful way to depict the nature of the divine agency involved in the event—which itself may be a narrative runtime for a historical episode that doesn't precisely match what we read in the Book of Exodus.

It may also be that our *anthro*pomorphizing of the divine is actually a backwards way of looking at the possibility that divinity has *theo*morphized us. That is, as beings capable of conscious engagement with the empirical, ethical, and esthetic code of the cosmos—and possessing agency in that coded cosmos—we may ourselves be analogs or images of the divine. That's not the worst possibility to consider as we attempt to live together in the world without destroying both it and ourselves.

26

A word about faith

Throughout this book, I've argued that we shouldn't be so quick to exclude the transcendent from the realm of the rational—nor to dismiss concepts of the divine as merely "matters of faith." I hope I've made a somewhat compelling argument that we can reason about such matters, despite the fact that they escape the limited scope of our scientific/empirical methods.

I'd now like to take a potshot at dualism from the opposite direction. It's not just that knowledge-stories about the transcendent can be subject to the same reason we use for science, history, and math. It's also that the single consciousness by which we engage with the world everyday isn't purely rational—and that faith is as much a component of consciousness as reason, no matter how much we may cringe at this claim.

First, let's deal with the word itself. "Faith" has a pretty broad range of meanings. It can be any kind of trust or belief. Webster's specifically calls out the kind of unquestioning belief associated with religious dogma—but even the most religious among us should be able to admit that their faith in dogma is often mixed with questions and uncertainties of one kind or another.

So, for our purposes here, let's keep our definition of "faith" broad enough to include confidence of any kind that is not fully based on empirical rigor alone. In other words, we exercise faith whenever we trust in something that has not been scientifically verified beyond a shadow of a doubt to be completely trustworthy.

Having lived in New Jersey for some time, for example, I would assert that driving on the NJ Turnpike requires the exercise of faith. No true New Jerseyan investigates highway safety statistics before deciding whether the risks of driving a particular stretch of turnpike at a particular time of day offset the benefits of a day on the Shore or a night in New York City. We simply get on at one exit and get off at another—trusting our fellow drivers to stay in their own lane, even if they're distracted or fatigued, even as we trust ourselves (rightly or wrongly) to drive safely.

Air travel also entails an exercise of faith. And, no, I don't mean faith in some magic force that keeps the aircraft aloft. I mean belief without empirical evidence that the pilot is mentally sharp, that the maintenance crew hasn't cut corners under time pressure, and that the manufacturer has been rigorous about the aircraft's construction. Everyone reading this who has traveled by air has had that faith confirmed. The passengers on the Boeing 737 MAX flights that crashed in 2018 and 2019 had their faith betrayed.

We exercise this conditioned faith constantly. We drink water from our taps and from plastic bottles, believing that someone somewhere is protecting its purity—despite the fact that we have absolutely no empirical evidence of that protection. If you live in Flint, Michigan, you know what it's like to have that faith shattered. But unless you're constantly paying to have your tap water tested, you're a person of faith when it comes to water quality.

I had a close friend who believed—with good reason—that he was the biological offspring of both his parents. He found out later in life that his parents had kept the truth from him. He had been caused to believe in a lie. But it's not as if any of us require our parents to submit to DNA testing to prove their paternity or maternity. My friend's belief-system was no different from my own. But my faith has not been proven (at least not as of this writing) to be misplaced. His was.

We exercise faith in our acceptance of knowledge-stories all the time. We trust teachers and authors. We watch a nature program on TV and take it on faith that their depiction of life in the wild is accurate. Never mind that they're splicing together clips to create a smooth narrative. Never mind that the story they tell may be based on somewhat thin anecdotal evidence. To us, such programs readily become our natural history gospel.

Speaking of history, how often do we trust such narratives from authoritative voices on faith alone? Do we have any choice? Few of us are in a position to do original research into the lives of lords and serfs in the Middle Ages. Nor does anyone I know own an actual time machine. So we trust others to both gather data for us and reasonably interpret that data. But we do so largely as a matter of faith—and not because we have personally observed their research or had them provide us with copies of all their original sources.

Even in the scientific community, there is a kind of trust that is not based on direct empirical evaluation. We trust researchers not to fudge their data or miscalibrate their instruments. This trust is often rewarded with useful insights about empirically observable phenomena. But that faith can also be misplaced. To say scientists who defraud us or make egregious errors are not "true scientists" is to fall victim to the "No True Scotsman" fallacy. Science is a human activity—and while it has some very strong safeguards (such as peer review and institutional oversight) against human foibles, it is in no way immune from them.

"Science" can be an especially convenient label for masking faith when it is used by non-scientists. There are those, for example, who put a great deal of stock in their own understanding of evolution— and have therefore turned the maxim "survival of the fittest" into a kind of dogma of their personal faith, despite the fact that, as we saw back in Chapter 18, it doesn't really mean anything.

Then there is the matter of the tremendous faith we place—often mistakenly—in our own intelligence and rationality. We'll consider this problem a bit more in the next chapter under the heading "Anosognosia." But suffice to say we all know what it's like to talk to someone who thinks they know what they're talking about when they don't. And, sad to say, we've all been that person ourselves.

Bottom line: We should probably dispense with the false duality of "reason" vs. "faith." ***When we exercise reason, we exercise faith in our ability to reason***—and when we exercise faith, we can exercise reason regarding the principles and objects of our faith. The human consciousness that grapples with the cosmos is not inherently divided into two realms. It may have multiple attributes, but those attributes are possessed by a single consciousness. The sooner we dispense with problematically dualistic models for that consciousness—and for the cosmos that our consciousness attempts to comprehend—the better.

27

For the skeptical

Some of you may have enjoyed the ride with me thus far. Some of you may merely be tolerating it. And some may be extremely skeptical. Is this Kahn guy running a con? Is he trying to slip one by me and get me to believe things I shouldn't rationally believe?

Well, yes and no. I am certainly trying to make a case for embracing the fullness of what human consciousness has to offer. And I'm using all the tricks of my trade as a writer to do so. But I believe I am doing so quite rationally, taking full advantage of the special insights newly afforded us by the pervasive and instructive phenomenon of software.

So for those of you who may find yourself resisting my arguments without being able to precisely put your finger on why, let me suggest a few *bad* reasons for doing so.

Ideational loyalty and affiliation

Over time, it can become more difficult for us to let go of long-held ideas. We start to identify strongly with certain ideas and with an in-group of those who hold those ideas with us. We also tend to become heavily invested in those ideas. We've argued passionately in their defense against those who disagree with us, online and in person. So surrendering those ideas can feel like a personal defeat.

This is as true for confirmed atheists[32] as it is for confirmed Baptists. We've held onto our ideas for so long, the gripping muscles of our intellect become many times stronger than the muscles that release.

Regarding this issue, one can only ask for an opening of the mind. A core attribute of the reasoning mind is the ability to adapt flexibly and appropriately to new insights and information. I would suggest that we have been granted genuinely new information in the form of software and its associated innovations—such as cloud computing, virtual hardware, and machine learning. I can only hope that this book offers some new insights in the context of that new information.

I believe this new information and insight provide a substantive basis for re-thinking one's ideas about the tangible and the transcendent. That re-thinking is a sign of mature rationality—not defeat or foolishness.

Chrono- and other -centrisms

Another common cause of resistance to new ideas is chronocentrism—a sort of unconscious preconceived notion that we have somehow reached the peak of knowledge in our present age. One only need read the writings of various times and places in human history to see the "arrogance of the present" on full display. Indeed, even a little ditty like "Kansas City" from the Rodgers and Hammerstein musical

---

[32] I actually find "atheist" to not be a very useful label. The word is as meaningless as "Christian"—which lumps together the most fundamentalist-literalist with those who read scripture critically and may actually be Deists. "Atheist" also only describes what one does *not* believe to be true—not what one affirmatively ascribes to. To disbelieve in gods as literally described in all their detail by religious dogmas may be entirely reasonable. To deny the transcendent entirely, as I believe I have reasonably argued, is not. One should therefore perhaps be cautious about identifying one's belief-system purely in terms of negation (i.e. rejection of anthropomorphic deities), when that negation could also imply full-blown anti-transcendence—which, as we have seen, is highly problematic.

Oklahoma! does a good job of satirizing the often-held opinion that the knowledge-keepers of our current age have "gone about as fer as they can go" when it comes to innovation and discovery.

But, of course, we know that this is not the case. Watson and Crick, for example, published their ground-breaking work on the double-helix structure of DNA back in 1953. But the mapping of the human genome wasn't declared complete until 2003—and we are still far from unraveling all of its mysteries.

We were pretty sure we had a working explanation of the cosmos, until we recognized the need for dark matter in our model. We were then pretty pleased with ourselves—until further investigation invalidated our models, and we found ourselves forced to theorize about dark energy.

The arrogance of the present extends to many of our ideas about history, society, and culture as well. Women couldn't vote as full citizens of the United States until the 19th Amendment was ratified in 1920. A century later, we're still grappling with workplace equality and other feminist principles. Then, too, we were pretty smug about our progress until the #MeToo movement came along, and we were forced to confront the realities of institutionalized male sexual misconduct towards women.

Excessive privileging of a narrowly empirical worldview can also devolve into ethnocentricity and racism. Those who discount the transcendent often wind up discounting much of non-Western culture. The transcendent belief-systems of other cultures do not inherently make them "ignorant" in a way that one's own "civilization" is not. We might, in fact, do well to learn from cultures that are less self-destructive—and less other-destructive—than the "enlightened" West has proven to be.

In other words, we should be cautious about thinking ourselves too fully evolved. We still have a long way to go. And the next step on that journey may entail re-thinking the transcendent aspects of ourselves and our universe based on new information afforded us by the software revelation.

Anosognosia

As a third caution, I'll introduce one of my favorite concepts: anosognosia. The neurologist Joseph Babinski coined the term in 1914 to refer to conditions in which a person with a mental disability is pathologically unaware of having it. It's a bit like denial—except with anosognosia you really, really can't perceive your own disability.

I'd suggest that we all have anosognosia to some degree. We simply cannot rationally claim to be perfectly rational—even if we're not sure in exactly which respects we are irrational. So we all need to have a certain healthy suspicion about our own thoughts and ideas. That's why I think it's reasonable to be skeptical about both out-of-hand rejection of transcendence and an easy dualism. And, yes, skepticism about the ideas offered in this book is healthy as well.

We should also be cautious about giving excessive credence to the assertions we or others make in one area of knowledge just because we or others possess impressive expertise in another. A world-famous epidemiologist may not be that astute when it comes to epistemology. A Nobel physicist may not be well-trained in metaphysics. Hubris can easily lead us into fallacy—especially in an online world teeming with misinformation and deceitful memes that try to get us to swallow bad ideas whole by falsely attributing them to Einstein, Gandhi, and Freud.

One of the great things about participating in a diverse community of rational thinkers is that we can examine each other for intellectual flaws—much as primates groom each other for bugs in their fur. Intellectually, all of us have hard-to-reach places where we cannot easily groom ourselves. Those are the spots where we must allow ourselves to be groomed, even as we do our best to charitably groom others. Perhaps for some of you the ideas put forth in this book can serve as an aid in such grooming. In any case, growth requires change—in our knowledge, our thinking, and our actions.

28

For the believer

A caution is also in order for those of us who enthusiastically embrace the transcendent—especially the ardent religionist. If you're one of these readers, you may find this book encouraging. And rightly so, since one of its core theses is that it is not inherently irrational to make assertions about the transcendent, the divine, or even a deity or deities.

By the same token, however, the arguments in this book impose a burden on "believers" to continually re-examine their beliefs in the clear light of reason. My arguments for including the transcendent in the rational is also an argument for including the rational in the transcendent.

In particular, I'll make the following suggestions to religionists who find the ideas in this book intriguing:

Reconsideration of dogma

Religions, sects, and other schools of thought regarding divinity all have their dogmas. Many of these dogmas are reasonable. Others are not. It's up to you, in consultation with those you consider to be sufficiently wise, to determine which is which.

It's certainly not my place to opine about the various dogmas of the world's religions—although I've probably tipped my spiritual hand a little. I will admit that I personally find feast- and fast-days to be a pretty reasonable way to bring individuals to mindfulness, while also promoting a healthy, tangible sense of relationality by making that mindfulness communal.

Other dogmas, on the other hand, seem to me to be obviously unreasonable. These include dogmas that demean individuals and groups inside and outside some particular faith community, that demand economic and/or political fealty, and that endow fallible human leaders with excessive authority.

It's unfortunate that questioning the dogmas of religion at times costs us membership in that religion's community. But, again, the intent of this book is not to tell clerics or congregants how to fulfill their roles. I know plenty of Catholics who are pro-choice and plenty of Jews who eat cheeseburgers. I am simply contending that individuals have the sovereign right to make rational choices about their personal belief-systems.

Narrative interpretation of sacred texts

Many religions and spiritual schools of thought are characterized by sacred texts that are central to their belief and practice. Such texts can serve a valuable purpose by providing a common point of reference for practitioners everywhere—ensuring a somewhat consistent "product" that is not overly distorted by the idiosyncrasies of dispersed local leadership.

In drawing from some of those sacred texts in this book, I've exercised my personal inclination to read certain passages as metaphorical code. Indeed, much of my college education entailed reading *all* language as semiotic coding that is subject to the runtime decoding of that language's interpreter.

Suffice to say that, given my understanding of language and the origin of texts, I find it reasonable to avoid the uncompromising literalism that so often undermines the reasonableness of religionists. Insisting so much on the letter of the text, to me, seems to frequently undermine the text's spirit. If you want to invest yourself wholly in an obviously non-literal creation myth, that's your choice. But there is a cost that needs to be weighed in making that choice.

Does that mean texts cannot be inspired? Of course not. Does it mean that there is no room for mystery or opacity in great writing? On the contrary, we probably need texts that disrupt our normative, everyday narrative to jar us into contemplation of the transcendent. This is what makes prophets and poets so essential to the human enterprise. As others have pointed out, it's not always rational for us to be too rational. We just have to be careful about being inappropriately counter-rational when it comes to the interpretation of texts.

Avoiding insularity

Another useful caution to the believer is to avoid excessive intellectual insularity. It is good to keep company with those who encourage us along our spiritual paths. And extended pursuit of a particular path with a guide who is deeply versed in that path can help keep us from becoming mere dilettantes of the transcendent.

We all, however, need to be cautious about surrounding ourselves only with people who agree with us. Excessive insularity is as counter-productive to growth as dilettantism. Neither offers us the antidote we all so sorely need to the anosognosia described in the previous chapter.

So my hope is not that this book offers you an alternative to your existing faith. My hope is that it enhances your embrace of the transcendent, regardless of the particular path you happen to be on at the moment.

If the divine is real, it must also have some logic (or some *logos*, if you will) to it. That logic, *logos*, order, or ur-code is definitely well beyond our immediate comprehension—but it exists nonetheless. Every religion was once a heresy. So we might all profit from listening to each other a little more.

■ ■ ■

One more note about religion. Religion isn't just about the ideas in our heads. It's about what we practice. It doesn't seem rational to me when we claim belief in peace while feeding a war machine or claim belief in love while neglecting the poor. So however we intellectualize the transcendent, we should all be careful not to think that thinking is all there is to it. Action is often the best crucible for reason. Let's not forget that—even as we study, contemplate, and debate.

29

The code of the cosmos

To close this section, let's break down the results of our reasoning thus far into four basic ideas:

1) **Software offers a useful model for transcendence.** By closely examining computer software, we've clearly seen that phenomena can have agency without having any directly observable existence. That's because software only consists of "values in relationship to each other." Those values and their relationality are abstractions that only become concrete when they are instantiated in runtimes at particular times and places.

   This model for transcendence doesn't just manifest in the case of computer software. We can find the same principle of agency-without-existence in many other types of encodings via values-in-relationship—including language, music, genetic code, and the underlying code of the material universe itself.

2) **The essence of the transcendent is relational.** Relationships can't be directly observed—but relationality is what gives the transcendent its identity and agency. We see this principle of _relational primacy_ in the sequential relationship between 0 and 1 values in software; in the relationships of pitch, time, and

volume between notes in a piece of music; and in the multi-dimensional relationships between people in society.

Even the cosmos itself is fundamentally relational—because it is built on underlying subatomic phenomena that are themselves a form of code. This relationality reveals itself empirically in everything from the way the relative mass and distance between two objects affect their gravitational attraction to the way observation of a quantum event is contingent upon its relation to the observer thereof.[33]

3) **We "read" the code of both the transcendent and the tangible as narrative.** To efficiently process the massive flood of data that we are bombarded with by an unimaginably complex cosmos, our minds must chunk that data into qualia-based narratives. This is why we distill the visual stimulus of light reflecting off the paint covering the main body of a car's exterior as "The car is red"—or describe the years-long process of a morally flawed but devastatingly handsome American-born male studying, researching, organizing, contemplating, and attempting to communicate thoughts about software and the divine by saying "That dude Kahn wrote a book."

---

[33] The "butterfly effect"—or the notion that everything in the universe is at least to some tiny degree relational to everything else—is wonderfully expressed in the concept of Indra's net, which is embraced by the Hua'yen school of Buddhism. According to this narrative, there is in the house of the goddess Indra a network of jewels so arranged that all reflect each other. This is just one way in which the sutras describe a universe in which every entity is not merely itself also an expression of every other entity.

Lest anyone mistakenly assume that universal relationality is an exclusively Eastern construct, however, I'll offer this advice from The Meditations of Marcus Aurelius, Section VI, #38: "Consider frequently the connection of all things in the universe and their relation to each other. For things are somehow implicated in each other, and all in a way friendly to one another; for one thing follows in order after another, and this is by virtue of their active movement and mutual agreement and the unity of their substance."

We become so comfortable with this use of chunked narrative that we can wind up confusing our functional narratives about the world with hard factual assertions about the reality of the world itself—assertions that could only be either fully true or fully false. But our narratives, while they can certainly be fully false, can rarely be said to be fully true. Even the most accurate map of the world is not the world. Our narratives can thus only be accurate to varying degrees. Human consciousness devises workable models for an underlying reality that we can at best only partially fathom.

4) **Even imperfect narratives can be useful.** The less-than-fully-accurate models we've used in the past to describe the physical universe were good enough for us to develop antibiotics and get human beings to the moon. The models we've developed more recently may also prove to be flawed—but that doesn't rob them of all utility. You don't need to know exactly how an internal combustion engine works to drive a car—and you don't need a degree in electrical engineering to change a light bulb. Imperfect knowledge can at times be sufficient knowledge.

The same is true of divine narratives. Narratives about God, gods, the human soul, love, beauty, and heroism may take great poetic liberty—but they are much more useful than no narrative at all. If we limit ourselves to narratives with a truth-rating of 10, we will hardly be able to make any knowledge claims at all. We can, of course, utterly deny our direct personal experience of consciousness. But that seems neither logical nor practical.

If you've been in love, if you've been moved by a piece of music, if the bright sun shining through the trees along a path through the woods has transported you to an inner state that sitting in your office cubicle does not, then an affirming narrative thereof has a higher truth-rating than a narrative that negates your experiences and/or claims that such experiences are absolutely and in all cases beyond our capacity for comprehension.

The transcendent is real—even if we struggle to pin it down. It's tough to pin anything down, actually. That's why human consciousness is not designed for pinning alone. That's why we constantly exercise faith in the face of uncertainty. And that's why our transcendent reach inevitably exceeds our tangible grasp.

PART VI:
SO WHAT?

(a/k/a POTENTIAL IMPLICATIONS OF THE SOFTWARE REVELATION)

30

An escape from dualism

Congratulations! You've made it through 29 chapters and 30,000 words of pretty challenging thought. And if you've made it this far, I've got some good news. The most difficult parts of this book are behind us. This last section merely considers some of the implications of the shift in thought that I've argued for based on what I believe software can reveal to us about how the universe works.

I'm not a consequentialist, though. I believe that if we uncovered anything true, that truth is itself inherently good—even if we can't immediately pin down any "practical results" that might arise as a result of discovering it.

That said, the following chapters nonetheless speculate about some positive outcomes that our "software revelation" might help bring about.

The first, as proposed at the outset of this work, is an escape from dualism. Dualism has been a concept of convenience for all types of thinkers over the centuries. For those who want to focus their energies exclusively on the material world, it has offered an expedient rationale for dismissing the transcendent. For religious thinkers, it has offered a handy excuse for dismissing the empirically problematic elements of their dogma. And for those who embrace both the tangible and the transcendent, it has offered an easy out for dismissing internal inconsistencies of reasoning.

As we have seen, however, by framing the cosmos as code—and framing consciousness as a sort of virtual machine—we can bring unity to our understanding of both the tangible and the transcendent. We don't have to posit two entirely separate realms of phenomena which require two entirely different modalities of knowledge: one of pure observation and reason, one of purely subjective experiential faith. We can posit a single human consciousness that processes a single cosmos through the single mechanism of narrative—which is as applicable to the science of ornithology as it is to poetizing about the eagle in flight.

I don't have two minds—one for studying empirical fact and one for doing the Electric Slide. There is one me that is conscious and does both.

Also, dualism depends on a false dichotomy about knowledge itself. Sure, we can choose to blithely place the mapping of the human genome squarely in one epistemic realm and arguments about social justice in another. But as we examine all realms of human inquiry, we find ourselves moving across a nuanced spectrum—rather than straddling a marked divide.

Inter-personal attraction, for example, has a biological component that is subject to empirical experiment. It also has psycho-social elements that are similarly subject to empirical study, although with somewhat less scientific precision. And there are aspects of inter-personal attraction that escape both the biologist and psychologist—instead yielding their mysteries more readily (although perhaps with less crystalline clarity) to the lyricist and playwright.

In other words, matters are not always purely clinical or purely esoteric. Much of life is an admixture of what we can see and what we can surmise. And all knowledge entails a measure of faith—whether that faith is placed in the knowledge-claims of experts, in the means by which we believe experts can rightly gain that knowledge, or in our own ability to receive that knowledge accurately and call it our own.

Does this mean that there are not distinct fields of knowledge? Of course not. There are many such fields, and most of us have more aptitude for some than for others.

But being better at numbers than words doesn't mean that word-consciousness is distinct from number-consciousness. We don't have countless disparate consciousnesses, even though there are countless fields of knowledge. We integrate our sight of the berry with our taste of the berry with our botanical knowledge about the berry. This integration is actually one of the most remarkable aspects of our consciousness. And the thoughtful co-mingling of diverse topics clearly enriches the active intellect, rather than fragmenting it.

Epistemic integration also explains why collaborations between experts in diverse fields can be so fruitful. CERN wasn't designed and built by a single person. It takes producers, actors, directors, cinematographers, sound engineers, and gaffers to make a movie. Even software requires a diversity of skills—including coding, interface design, user acceptance testing, and security assurance. We complement each other with our differing knowledge, experiences, and skills.

So perhaps we can dispense with dualism. It seems neither empirically nor logically viable. And the model of encoding-and-runtime offers us a clear and compelling alternative.

31

Relief from reductive materialism

Software offers us a coherent model for understanding transcendence. It does this by radically shifting our focus from tangible stuff to relationality—even though we can't directly observe relationality or always pin it down in all of its particulars.

This radical shift is appropriate because, as we noted in Chapter 12, there are many, many more relationships between things than there are things. Or, as I sometimes like to put it, ***there's a lot more space between stuff than there is stuff.***[34]

Another potential benefit of our "software revelation" is therefore relief from reductive materialism.

Reductive materialism is the belief that the material world is all there is. Many of us ascribe to this belief either consciously or unconsciously. We therefore treat assertions about the transcendent—that is, anything other than tangible matter and energy—as speculative at best and sheer bunk at worst.

---

[34] I am tempted to invoke Derrida here, especially as he discusses presence and absence—as well as what he calls "traces" and the movement of linguistic signifiers into empty spaces. Any direct quotation from his work might be too opaque for this book, but if you can make your way through his Positions, he does say some pretty cool stuff about "the systematic play of differences, of the traces of differences, of the spacing by means of which elements are related to each other."

Reductive materialism manifests itself in a variety of associated belief-systems. These include scientism (i.e. the notion that only the scientific method can yield knowledge), various brands of atheism (including outright anti-transcendence), and nihilism.[35]

It's understandable that many of us would lapse into such materialism. Our continually expanding scientific knowledge has falsified much religious dogma. And religious institutions, for their part, have often resisted new knowledge—thereby forfeiting much of their epistemic credibility. Faced with a choice between largely credible science and less-than-totally credible religious dogma, many of us have gone "all in" with the former.

For others, however, reductive materialism has felt like a stone in humankind's metaphysical shoe—forcing us to throw out the transcendent baby with the dogmatic bathwater. As we become more dismissive of the rites, rituals, texts, and God-narratives of specific religions, we can find ourselves left with nothing but vague personal beliefs about "something more."

And we're often not even sure how to defend those personal beliefs against the sharp blade of exclusionary scientistic logic. So we can feel as pressured to conform with the dogma of reductive materialism as a monk of the Middle Ages might have been to conform with the catechism of the Roman Catholic Church.

Here's where our software-based arguments regarding transcendence-as-relationality can offer relief. If computer software can have empirically observable agency without possessing empirically observable being, so can something else—whether that something else is a god, a soul, or the experiential impact of a blazing sunset.

---

[35] For a good overview of alternatives to purely reductive materialism, consider reading *Physicalism Deconstructed* by Ken Morris (Cambridge University Press, 2019), which offers a useful overview of non-reductive physicalism, non-skeptical eliminative physicalism, and other branches of contemporary phenomenology.

And when a reductive materialist (or even our own nagging Spock-like inner voice of erstwhile "logic") tells us we are irrational for assigning a truth-rating of more than zero to such transcendence, we can reply with software-inspired (and perhaps Kirk-like) confidence that it would be irrational *not* to embrace the relational narratives of our own consciousness.

Does this give us license to promulgate whatever nonsense we choose about the "spiritual" or "supernatural" simply by claiming our subjective right to do so? Of course not. Reason always counts. But a clear understanding of our new software-based principles—especially the principle of *relational primacy*—can help us more rationally frame our conscious experience of both the tangible and the transcendent. An understanding of what I've termed "the software revelation" may also help us better communicate our ideas about the transcendent with one another.

32

Re-thinking performative individualism

Some people accomplish seemingly great things and are recognized for it. We heap great attention on the movie star, the superior athlete, and the accumulator of vast wealth.

But are the lives of these people of greater inherent value than the competent plumber or the devoted schoolteacher? And what of those who are physically or psychologically challenged in ways that limit what they can do? Is there some objective, empirical reason for us to value any of these individual's lives more or less than another's?

This is not a trivial question. Many of us have internalized a value-system that places Alexander the Great at the top of a performance pyramid and a homeless crack addict on the bottom. But if we truly believe that the scale upon which we can each be judged is based on our individual fame, wealth, power, or accomplishment, then being human is largely about trying to muddle vainly through a temporary and mediocre existence while ignoring our failure to perform in comparison to some idealized elite. Or, as an alternative strategy, we may decide to only compare ourselves to those further down the imagined performance scale than we are—while we fearfully avoid looking in the other direction.

This notion of a human performance scale informs many aspects of our life-narratives. Some who oppose abortion rights or favor more open immigration policies, for example, support their arguments by invoking the possibility that a person who could potentially discover a cure for cancer or achieve some other great thing might be prevented from being born or from entering the country.

Similarly, we often encourage children to pursue their education not for its own sake, but because they can "be anything they want to be"—which tacitly implies becoming President of the United States or the next Steve Jobs or some other supposedly laudable personage.

Such idealizations ring false and are probably counter-productive. A day laborer who gives an honest hour's work for an honest hour's pay, is a helpful neighbor, and rigorously avoids harming others is no less a human being than the political machinator who lies and schemes and creates a massive carbon footprint on the way "up." If we are disappointed in children of high moral integrity because they have not sought and gained the upper-middle-class lifestyle we covet, then it is we who are poor—not them. And if the only life worth living is one that earns a half-hour spot on a cable TV show, then there is good reason for the rest of us to be anxious and depressed.

The software revelation can offer some relief from this culture of performative individualism by suggesting two things. First, it suggests that human life is of value not only because it is merely biologically alive, but because it is conscious. It is capable of encoding and runtime—which is pretty spectacular if you think about it. Whether an individual achieves top-dog status through a combination of effort and luck is secondary at best. Every human being is non-trivially differentiated from mere matter by virtue of their ability to participate in the transcendent—which we do whether we explicitly think of ourselves as doing so or not.

Second, as code processors, human beings are inherently networked with other human beings—and with the broader cosmos. This means that our role in the universe is not just as individual "atomic" entities, but as part of a web of complex relationality. The tycoon depends on the road worker who depends on the bureaucrat who depends on the taxpayer and so on. Hierarchical models of human societies may thus be less appropriate than network maps.

The COVID-19 pandemic offered a dramatic illustration of how interdependent we all are. Unless you grow your own food, the grocery worker is as critical to your survival—and the survival of your entire community—as any business executive or politician. The more in touch we are with this reality, the more likely our social and political discourse will be based in reality, rather than falsifiable dogmas.

We are genuinely a "we." And cooperation is at as vital an evolutionary advantage as physical strength or technical smarts.

As the poet John Donne wrote:

> *No man is an island,*
> *Entire of itself.*
> *Each is a piece of the continent,*
> *A part of the main.*
> *If a clod be washed away by the sea,*
> *Europe is the less.*
> *As well as if a promontory were.*
> *As well as if a manor of thine own*
> *Or of thine friend's were.*
> *Each man's death diminishes me,*
> *For I am involved in mankind.*
> *Therefore, send not to know*
> *For whom the bell tolls,*
> *It tolls for thee.*

In a way, it's ironic that an understanding of software-inspired transcendence may help us better understand ourselves as inherently inter-connected and inter-dependent—because there's a strong strain of performative individualism in tech culture. During my many sojourns in Silicon Valley, I've encountered proponents of what is popularly referred to as "The Quantified Self." The idea behind The Quantified Self is that by using apps to monitor and measure various aspects of our individual lives, we can improve them. Devotees of this movement adopt metrics for their biological health, their business productivity, and the like—with the aim of optimizing their performance as individuals.

One question I usually ask proponents of this model is "What's your ethical metric?" It's a question they have not yet shown themselves equipped to answer. That's because ethical performance does not readily lend itself to metrics. But if you believe, as I do, that ethical behavior is a primary aspect of the human endeavor—that the relational aspect of our lives is central to who we are—then it doesn't really make sense to constantly measure ourselves against a numeric scorecard of individual achievement. There is something much more to being human.

What a relief! How liberating it is to not be in some unforgiving zero-sum footrace against my fellow-beings. My job is to be me—to play my personal role as best I can in a relational cosmos where we all depend on each other to enable the unfolding of a shared future.

We are individuals. That's obvious. But we live together, as will our children and our children's children. Embracing the reality of our profound and transcendent relationality seems much more rational than pretending we are all on our own solo flights through an ethical vacuum.

33

Towards more relational economics

It's all well and good to muse about God, truth, and beauty. But while we do so, we must live in a material world where food, shelter, and clothing cost money—and we are all therefore actively engaged in the getting and spending thereof.

To aid us in this endeavor, we turn to economics and economists. Economics helps us measure, analyze, and even predict how markets work, how people make financial decisions, and how government policies can affect the lives of citizens. Economists help us do economics.

Unfortunately, economics has historically not been very relational. That is, it has examined and measured economic behaviors in a highly siloed manner. A classic example of this is transactional externality. A business sells a product for ten dollars. The cost to the business to produce this product—including all materials, labor, energy, distribution, marketing, overhead, etc.—is nine dollars. In the simplest terms, the business reaps a profit of one dollar. If the business can repeat this transaction often enough, it will make a profit. It may also be rewarded by investors with a certain valuation.

This simple formula, however, does not factor in realities that are external to the transaction itself. What impact does the manufacture and distribution of the product have on the environment? Does the sale of the product adversely impact the economics of some adjoining businesses or professions? Will the continued use of the product impose some other cost on society? By ignoring these externalities, atomistic economics can distort decision- and policy-making in detrimental ways.

In fact, without the right relational context, virtually all economic metrics are deceiving. A year-over-year improvement in wage growth, for example, can sound like good news. But it's not really good news for wage-earners if the cost of housing is growing at a faster rate. A rise in a stock market index can also sound like an indicator of economic health. But the expectations of a few money managers that a handful of companies will attract greater investment in the near future is not an indicator that the children of the poor are being fed any better.

The software revelation cannot, of course, remedy this shortcoming in our economics all by itself. But by highlighting the relational nature of human existence, it can suggest that economists more carefully consider the connections between individual market metrics and the entire network of participants in our shared economic life, between wealth concentrated in one node on that network and the circulation of life-sustaining money flows across all paths on which other nodes reside.

There's an analog to this in computing. Early computing architectures concentrated all the code-running capabilities in the world on a relatively few machines—leaving users at so-called "dumb" terminals that didn't run any code at all, but simply sent input and received output from centralized mainframes. That model didn't take us very far.

Eventually, though, we learned that it was far better to democratize code by putting previously unthinkable code-processing power directly into the hands of even computer-illiterate end-users. And the results have been extraordinary. Code is now pervasive, and we can use it to improve many more aspects of life than we could under the old model.

We even distribute our centralized computing power across large numbers of virtual machines in hives of cloud-based processors. Distribution has simply proven itself to be more efficient, effective, and resilient than excessive concentration.

This is not to say that what is good for computing is automatically good for finance. But it is worth considering the parallels between all types of code—computer code, naturally occurring code, the divine ur-code, and the "code" that is money. The optimum outcome of centuries of collective human consciousness is probably not a single extremely wealthy individual. Nor is it likely extreme poverty for the many. By better understanding our relationality we may reach more rational and ethically coherent conclusions about our economic policies and practices.

It may, in fact, be wise to better frame economics itself within the overall context of the human experience. We say "Money can't buy happiness"—and then go on to act as if it does. Studies show that Latin American countries such as Colombia and Guatemala, for example, score higher on polls of personal emotional happiness than Nordic countries such as Finland and Sweden, which rank higher in purely economic metrics such as per-capita GDP.

And who's to say that self-reported happiness is the ultimate metric for a life well-lived? If I happily mistreat people and abuse the environment, am I really running the code of the cosmos all that well?

Despite the fact that we know these things intuitively, we nonetheless continue to report the rise and fall of narrowly calculated market indices on a daily basis as if they were the prime indicators of the nation's present condition. Why not a daily reporting on the number of suicides or homicides? Or a self-reporting of how many good deeds we've done?

Our software revelation may not induce us to adopt such novel relational metrics for the quality of life on our planet. But perhaps a software-inspired worldview can at least get us to start questioning the many existing economic metrics and practices that mislead us and undermine our collective quality of life.

34

Balancing self and society

The software revelation helps us understand that reality is primarily relational, despite the fact that we cannot directly observe relationships themselves. It can therefore serve as a useful corrective to our tendency to view our interpersonal relationships as secondary to our individual selves.

Or, to again re-purpose our phrase from Chapter 12, there are many, many more relationships between people than there are people.

This understanding of human society can be helpful in many ways. At a theoretical level, for example, we are often presented with a false either/or choice between two extremes. At one extreme is the total subjugation of the individual to the whole. This wholly collectivist model of society is familiar to us in the caricatures of the totalitarian Communist state or the oppressive authoritarianism of the medieval Catholic Church.

On the other extreme is the unbridled exaltation of the individual. We see this thread of extreme individualism wind its way from the Reformation and the Enlightenment through the emergence of Western liberal democracies.

Absolute collectivism is obviously problematic. If we deny the individual, we deny our direct experience of personal consciousness. And by repressing the exercise of individual choice and creativity, absolute collectivism also denies society the full potential giftings of the individuals who comprise that society.

Absolute individualism, though, is also problematic—especially as it manifests in the conscious or unconscious embrace of Randian objectivism. As observers like Gertrude Himmelfarb have pointed out, excessive preoccupation with our personal, individual quality of life undermines the shared economic and social foundations which make such self-centered preoccupation possible. Or, as George Eliot wrote, unbounded exaltation of the individual can cause us to slide decadently into "taking the world as an udder to feed our supreme selves."[36]

There is, of course, an alternative to both of these extremes. We are certainly individuals. But as individuals, we inherently exist in relationship to other individuals and to our environment. Software teaches us that these relations are not secondary to our individualism. They are actually the very stuff of our individual identities and our individual agency.

I am not first an individual and secondly an individual in relation to others. _Relational primacy_ reveals that it is the unique combination and quality of my relations that make me uniquely me. It is where I was born, who I was born to, what I was taught, how I absorbed it, what was done to me, and how I have treated others that make me me.

If we look at how we describe others, we can see that their attributes as individuals are likewise relational attributes. Do you describe someone as "tall?" That obviously means they are tall relative to other people—not relative to a blade of grass or a skyscraper. Do you describe them as "friendly" or as someone who "kinda keeps to themselves?" Those are also clearly relational descriptions.

Our moral measures—whatever they may be—are similarly relational. We call serial killers "evil" because of the harm they've inflicted on

---

[36] _Middlemarch_, Part II, Chapter 21

others, not because of the pathological thoughts in their heads or any misery they may have caused themselves. We call the philanthropist "good" because of financial generosity towards the needy, not because of their pleasant thoughts about life or their indulgence of their own personal appetites. Gluttony is only gluttony because it entails consumption that is disproportionate in relation to others. Envy is negative because it entails a distorted perspective regarding the good experienced by someone other than oneself.

The personal relationality is highly analogous to the relationality of the software we use every day. The app I enjoy on my smartphone is very nicely coded. It is a work of great craft executed by a team of developers. But the excellence of their coding is particularly revealed in how easily and securely that app can connect with a payment system that connects to my bank account—and how seamlessly all those apps communicate with each other over wired and wireless networks. The capability of an app is highly contingent upon the quality of its relationships with other software across multiple networks and sub-networks. And the quality of those relationships is contingent upon how well each application is coded for relationality—i.e., its ability to interface with other code—especially vis-à-vis the operating system and other software on my smartphone.

The software revelation can thus potentially have a positive influence on society by helping us to better balance our understanding of ourselves as both individual and relational. We all at times experience feelings of isolation and alienation. But the reality is that we all belong. And that belonging is deeply intrinsic to our very being.

This belonging—this synergy between the individual and the relational—is more than just a psychological comfort or a philosophical thought-exercise. A strong sense of relationality is essential if we are to act collectively even as we live individually. And if we cannot act collectively, our very survival is at risk.

35

A final word

Software is powerful and pervasive. But it has no empirically observable existence, because it lives in the spectral relationships between values. The transcendent aspects of our universe similarly escape our direct observation because they, too, live in an immaterial relationality.

The invisibility of the transcendent in no way renders it less powerful or pervasive than that which we can empirically detect. In fact, just the opposite is true. Relationality makes things what they are—and it endows them with their agency.

Or, to once again re-phrase the principles of _relational primacy_ that is at the heart of the software revelation, **everything that happens happens between.**

This seemingly abstract metaphysical notion has concrete, valuable implications. Abstract ideas often do. The ideas of money, of the nation-state, of race, of evolution, of relativity, and of God have all certainly had an impact on the world—whether for better, worse, or some combination of the two.

So what happens when we recognize that our world is primarily transcendent relationality, rather than a bunch of tangible stuff? How might it influence our thinking (and, by extension, our actions) when we realize that software—this phenomenon we've created out of nothing but invisible 0s and 1s, yet that now so pervasively affects our lives—is a model for the transcendent?

And how might that software-inspired re-thinking be reinforced by the realization that code has always been with us in the form of language, music, genetics, and the fundamental composition of the cosmos itself?

My hope is that this book has encouraged you to ask yourself these questions. I've proposed a few answers. They include the suggestions that we can fully embrace the transcendent while being fully rational, that we can put aside dualism and accept that all of our truth-assertions—whether scientific or mythical—possess a certain metaphorically narrative quality, and that we become more intentional about connecting with each other and with our environment.

But my personal attempt at answering these questions is far less important than the questions themselves. In fact, it is my hope that your answers will be better than mine. My job has simply been to point out something I've glimpsed through decades of intensive engagement with software, science, religion, language, music, and metaphysics. I may have not done that job very well, but now it's done—and it is in your hands.

One thing I am fairly sure of. The transcendent and our direct experiences of the transcendent are real. We don't have to doubt our own reasonableness or sanity just because we ascribe high truth-ratings to our narrative assertions about these invisible realities. Empirical inquiries and transactional outcomes are not the sole means by which we can rightly comprehend the temporary but rich lives of conscious human experience that we have been granted. Our understanding can expand and evolve—even as it builds on that of our forebears.

My narrative-of-choice at present describes that expanded, evolved understanding in terms of code, transcendence, relationality, and the divine. But let's not marry ourselves to words. Let's marry ourselves to the questions—or, perhaps more accurately, to the quest—and see where it takes us.

Acknowledgements

There isn't enough space here to acknowledge all those who have been generous enough to share their knowledge and wisdom with me in the classroom, through the printed word, online, and in private conversation. But I would be remiss if I didn't at least try to name some names of those who have contributed the education of a curious child. These names include Irene Taylor, Virginia Schechet, Robert Handschuh, Rabbi Barry Schaeffer, Robert Farris Thompson, Stanley Weinstein, Leopold Pospisil, J. Hillis Miller, J.D. McClatchy, Charles Berger, Bishop Seraphim Sigrist, Pastor Phil Raynis, Carlos Dalmau, Irving Wladawsky-Berger, Tim Berners-Lee, Nick Smart, Peter Gardner, Brandon Ehrfurth, and Dr. Jeffrey Ellias-Frankel.

And of course infinite thanks to Mom, Dad, my big sister, my two incomparable sons, and the rest of the family—who have always encouraged me to learn, think, argue, and write.

Printed in the United States
By Bookmasters